Ye Shall Dream

Ye Shall Dream

PATRIARCH GRANVILLE WILLIAMS AND THE BARBADOS SPIRITUAL BAPTISTS

Ezra E.H. Griffith

UNIVERSITY OF THE WEST INDIES PRESS
Jamaica • Barbados • Trinidad and Tobago

University of the West Indies Press
7A Gibraltar Hall Road Mona
Kingston 7 Jamaica
www.uwipress.com

CATALOGUING-IN-PUBLICATION DATA

Griffith, Ezra E.H., 1942–
Ye shall dream : Patriarch Granville Williams and the Barbados Spiritual Baptists / Ezra E.H. Griffith.

p. cm.

Includes bibliographical references.

ISBN: 978-976-640-242-6 (cloth)
ISBN: 978-976-640-243-3 (paper)

1. Williams, Granville. 2. Spiritual Baptists – Barbados. 3. Blacks – Barbados – Religion. 4. Christian sects – Barbados. 5. Sons of God Apostolic Spiritual Baptist Church (Barbados). 6. Barbados – Religious life and customs. I. Title.

BX9798.S6535B348 2010 289.9

Book and cover design by Robert Harris.
Set in Adobe Garamond 11/14.5 x 24
Printed in Canada.

To Patriarch Granville Williams
and past and present members of the
Sons of God Apostolic Spiritual Baptist Church of Barbados

You welcomed me into your midst and gave me freedom to pursue my scholarly interests in your doctrine and rituals. I thank you for all your kind and gracious help. I take humble responsibility for my observations and analyses and pray that in them you see fairness and a profound respect for your faith and traditions.

AND

To the Reverend Marlene Stewart,
a patient sister in Christ

You conducted Bible class in person and by telephone, forcing me to go back and turn those pages of my King James Version so often they now have permanent "dog-ears".

Contents

Foreword

JONATHAN SCOTT HOLLOWAY

HUMANS ARE SOCIAL CREATURES. We navigate our worlds seeking out collaborations – be they family, friend or stranger – hoping to find those who will help us secure comfort and perhaps even joy. As we are unpredictable creatures, these relationships are in a constant state of negotiation. We discover love, we experience betrayal, we act altruistically, we distort things to gain advantage, we develop skills, we rediscover old truths, we lie awake at night chased by demons of our making, and we dream. There is nothing new in these observations, of course, but we too rarely stop to ponder our passage.

Let's face it; it is difficult to take everything in. After all, so much of our lives is pursued without having or taking the time for thoughtful reflection. Technology allows us to do ever more, but it also distracts us from finding the time for the kind of quiet reflection we need in order to process our social needs with clear minds. We chase after new opportunities that will promise us greater material comfort, at least until the next "latest thing" is unleashed upon the public and then, a short while later, goes on sale. We seek fulfilment, but technological change tells us in so many matter-of-fact ways that we will never be complete. Thus we continue on, ever hopeful that next time everything will be just right. It is as if we are continually running, sometimes with discipline but often amok, toward an elusive goal, only rarely aware that the only way to get to that goal is by slowing down and walking.

For many of us, the one certain time each week when we do unplug long enough to listen to the silence in our lives and reflect upon it comes during religious services. The weekly gathering time helps us navigate our social worlds and reaffirm at least one type of community. The slow pace of change in religious practices is itself reassuring. Although there are any number of issues that come before our faith communities that cry out for change, if only for the sake of humanity, we would be foolish to deny the fact that the predictability of so many practices is the one thing that many of us need in order to gird ourselves up for the challenges of our frenzied world. It is as if we get to say, "On this day, I know what to expect and this calms me and helps me be at peace."

But really, little if anything that I offer here amounts to a new observation. After all, humanity's unpredictability and religion's predictability are known and are familiar. What are we to make, then, of this book? On its surface, after all, Ezra Griffith's *Ye Shall Dream: Patriarch Granville Williams and the Barbados Spiritual Baptists* is a book rich with these kinds of observations. *Ye Shall Dream* examines the social and religious practices of individuals who, on the whole, lead quiet and simple lives. They work, they play, they love and laugh, they conjure and misdirect, they practise their faith, and they (mostly) abide by the rules of Patriarch Granville Williams and the Sons of God Apostolic Spiritual Baptist Church.

With his steady hand guiding us along, Griffith navigates this world. His warm and inviting narrative lets us accompany him into the Spiritual Baptists' houses of worship, listen to the bells and moans of service, see the rich colours and textures of the vestments, follow the worshippers to the water for baptism, and develop a rich appreciation for the roles that the mundane (the order and hierarchy of the Church) and the fantastic (the significance of dreams) play in this community.

By his implicit request that we follow his lead and slow down, Griffith does what all great ethnographers do: he makes the reader switch places with the "subject". That is, the reader becomes the "alien" and the community under study becomes the norm. Through *Ye Shall Dream,* the hyper-secularized and hyper-caffeinated reader can recognize in those presumptively "less developed" communities entire sets of social, cultural and ethical commonalities. The net effect of this discovery is that our notion of community grows and our assumption about what is worth knowing and understanding expands as well. We can see with freshly opened eyes – as if we had awakened from our own slumber fuelled by dreams of material accumulation and speed, ever more speed – that there are other highly functional social and cultural logics that might enrich our lives if we only stopped to consider them.

All of this is not to say that Griffith's study is mere celebration. Not by a long shot. Indeed, much of the grace and dignity one finds in *Ye Shall Dream* springs from the fact that Griffith allows the Barbadians he studies to be fully human. He shows us that the Spiritual Baptists are not archetypes who are above their own frailties. There is order among the faithful, but there is confusion as well. There is love, but envy is proximate. More than anything else, however, Griffith shows us that the Spiritual Baptists possess a commitment to something greater than the individual. Most significantly, it is "this greater thing" that enhances the quality and meaning of life – not Life 2.0 that can be downloaded wirelessly while waiting for the latest consumptive interpretation that ground cacao beans might yield, but life guided by a spiritual faith that there is meaning in tradition, meaning in order, and, even though always mysterious, meaning in dreams.

Acknowledgements

AFTER SO MANY YEARS of pursuing these scholarly efforts, I'm still awed by the number of people who must support university professors in order to help them produce their written scholarship. This text is no exception. Jacqueline Coleman, Victor Rogers, Elwin Griffith, Michael Clarke and Edith Jacobs read early versions of the manuscript. Brigitte Jung gave sustained attention to the later version, as did John Young, a devoted colleague. Jonathan Holloway and his graduate students at Yale reviewed the manuscript and engaged me in almost two hours of vibrant and incisive discussion of my work. Sean Agard and Elma Cumberbatch repeatedly answered my questions and helped me focus my eyes to see and my ears to hear rituals that at first seemed so foreign. Madelon Baranoski and Larry Davidson, astute Yale colleagues, provided invaluable advice about methodology. George Mahy and John Young were collaborators in early work about the Barbados Spiritual Baptists. I thank them all most earnestly. Those who so graciously served as my "informants" deserve my thanks, as they played a major part in this narrative, even if I cannot name them. And the work would never have progressed without the aesthetic contributions of Mark Saba and Felix Kerr. They helped me bring out the performative beauty of the Barbados Spiritual Baptists. Unless otherwise noted, the photographs presented in the text, along with the cover photo, were taken by me. The photo facing page 1 and the one at the end of chapter 3 were graciously contributed by the Patriarch.

Ceremonial greeting of fellowship and unity between members of the Spiritual Baptist Church. (Photo from the collection of Patriarch Granville Williams.)

CHAPTER 1

Framing the Narrative

RELIGION IS AN IMPORTANT cultural element in the English-speaking Caribbean, and nowhere could this be more evident than on the island of Barbados. On this relatively small 144 square miles of land, religious institutions have enjoyed a long and vibrant history. They have participated in educational, health, political and other socio-cultural activities over an extended period of time. The religious organizations carrying out this activity on the island have generally been white-dominated or have been offshoots of white-dominated faith groups. An exception to this trend has been the Sons of God Apostolic Spiritual Baptist Church, which was founded in Barbados by a black Barbadian named Granville Williams when he returned to the island in 1957 after living in Trinidad. This book is the story of this unique religious group and its founder.

I became acquainted with the Barbados Spiritual Baptists a little over twenty-five years ago when a member of the group introduced one of my colleagues and me to the group's founder and the Church services. At the time, I had expressed an interest in studying a religious group on the island. This curiosity had developed from my clinical observations that a certain group of psychiatric patients frequently seemed to colour their symptomatic complaints with religiously tinged language and behaviour. At first, these observations led me to study Puerto Rican patients and their indigenous religious system called Espiritismo (Griffith and Ruiz 1977). From there I turned to an examination of patients who used a church-based clinic in Jamaica that offered psychiatric, medical and prayer services in a tripartite model (Griffith 1983). Then I wondered about the Spiritual Baptist group I was hearing so much about in Barbados, the Caribbean island where I was born and raised.

In those early years after the group was founded, the Barbados Spiritual Baptists were seen by the broader community as a cult group, with strange religious rituals and a belief system that boggled the minds of the unbelievers. My colleagues and I were curious about how members of the group melded their faith and their secular lives, especially in relation to taking care of their health needs. In other words, we were curious about the notion that, in their own way, the Barbados Spiritual Baptists might very well be serving as an effective healing community for a cross-section of the Barbadian society.

As I continued my observations of the Church group over the years, the originally narrow conceptual view of the Barbados Spiritual Baptists grew into a broader therapeutic notion: the organization had an impact on its members (for the most part Afro-Barbadian) that made them feel better about themselves through the development and maintenance of a distinctively special relationship with God. This idea that the group could have a therapeutic impact on its members was multi-dimensional. In the course of our work, my colleagues and I noted that some members talked about participation in Church rituals that had a relief effect on their mood. Others said that the Church gave them a clearer sense of their connection to Africa and who they were. Still others said that the Church made them more confident about themselves and facilitated their interest in being more outgoing and self-confident (Griffith and Mahy 1984; Griffith, Mahy and Young 1986).

At the same time, I gradually recognized that little scholarly work had been done on this group in comparison to observations written about the Trinidad and Tobago Spiritual Baptists. (For recent work, see, for example, Henry 2003; Laitinen 2002; Lum 2000.) What was therefore needed was an ethnographic report on the Barbados Spiritual Baptists with an eye to shedding light on their practices and the mechanisms used by the group in pursuit of this therapeutic end. Such an ethnography could open an important window onto this community, which, after well over fifty years, is now enjoying broad acceptance by the secular society. In turn, knowledge of the Spiritual Baptists should provide a significant vantage point for understanding other cultural developments in post-independence Barbadian society. One additional point to make is that the Spiritual Baptists were an important subject of conversation wherever I went in Barbados in the early 1980s. Few people actually knew much about them, however, and not a single one of my friends had ever attended service at one of their Churches, although people had seen the group conducting open-air services in the bus stand. So conversations about the group were often full of fantasy and jocular distortion. This work is a contribution to filling the vacuum and providing information about the Church, its doctrine and its rituals.

As several authors (Simpson 1966; Guglin 1974) have pointed out, Spiritual Baptists believe in one God, Jesus Christ and baptism by immersion in a body of living water. They also subscribe to the authenticity of biblical miracles and possession by the Holy Spirit. They communicate regularly with God through the media of visions and dreams. Some distinctive features of the Spiritual Baptists are their uniquely rhythmic manner of singing, their common use of candles in ceremonies, and their sacred respect of the lota (a brass vessel containing water, leaves and flowers placed around a lighted candle). Once baptized and welcomed into the Church, members usually attend services wearing robes that vary in colour and have Spiritual Baptist symbols embroidered on them. Both male and female members may have their heads covered in Church services. Men may wear towels tied around their heads or head apparel often seen in Catholic or Anglican rituals, such as the three-pointed biretta. Women wear scarves of assorted colours and shapes that are tied in different configurations. In Barbados, the scarves used to tie the heads of female members have been so striking and unusual that their appearance quickly gave birth to the name "The Tie-Heads".

The Spiritual Baptists' most unusual ritual is their practice called "mourning". This activity is based on the biblical description of Daniel's having mourned three weeks (Daniel 10). Simpson (1966), Ward and Beaubrun (1979), and Griffith and colleagues (Griffith and Mahy 1984; Griffith, Mahy and Young 1986) have described the ceremony in which mourners are isolated in a special area of the Church, with their eyes and ears covered so as to eliminate or minimize sensory stimulation. This practice continues usually for a period of seven days or longer. During the mourning period, the individual fasts, is constantly in a state of prayer, and frequently experiences dreams and visions. At the end of the mourning period, the mourners recount their spiritual travels to the whole congregation in a service expressly organized for that purpose. As I will explicate later, the results of mourning experiences can have a substantive effect on an individual's standing in the Church and on how other members view that individual member's degree of spirituality.

The Barbados Spiritual Baptist Church is an example of a religious movement that was initially introduced to the island just over fifty years ago. Griffith, Mahy and Young (2008) have argued that the Church has undergone transformation from a disparaged religious cult into a settled and accepted denomination. This transformation is an essential step toward conceptualizing the future roles that this particular faith group may be able to play in Barbados and throughout the Caribbean.

It is essential that we understand what factors may have facilitated Granville Williams's success in having the Church establish strong roots at the time of his return to the island. I have previously argued (Griffith 1992) that Williams returned at a time when the island was a British colony and the black population was suffering from material deprivation, economic hardship and a pervasive sense of hopelessness about its future. I suggested that Williams set out new possibilities for the black underclass when he offered new strategies for redefining its sense of self. For example, he evoked the idea that Jesus was black and that blacks could fashion their own relationship to God without resorting to the rituals utilized by European colonizers. Williams suggested that in this new religious movement (by which I mean new to Barbados), spiritual mysteries that were not revealed to the white colonial masters would be accessible to those who were willing to follow him and hear the true word of God. In the trappings of the Spiritual Baptist movement, Williams seized the chance to promote a religious ritual and belief system with pronounced African trends in it, and thereby to improve the lot of black Barbadians.

This is not to suggest that Williams did it all singlehandedly. As Griffith and colleagues (2008) have pointed out, there were other forces at work, as is often the case in such developments. Barbados became independent of Great Britain in 1966, a short decade after Williams's return. At the same time, the Black Power movement was sweeping Europe and North America and being noticed in the Caribbean with the new emphasis on Afro hairstyles and dashikis. The struggle over South African Apartheid was being discussed everywhere, including its meaning on the cricket field (Beckles 1998). In the Caribbean, debates were vigorously focused on definitions of self-identity and group identity. This terrain contributed powerfully to the relevance of Granville Williams.

Besides those already mentioned, other scholars have also described the Spiritual Baptist movement in Trinidad (see, for example: Simpson 1966, 1980; Ward and Beaubrun 1979; Glazier 1983; Jacobs 1996). Henney (1982) focused her attention on the group in St Vincent, and Duncan (2008) has recently published work on the Spiritual Baptists in Toronto, Canada. Less sustained scholarly attention has been brought to bear on the group in Barbados, however. My colleagues and I have carried out previous work on the Barbados Spiritual Baptists (Griffith and Mahy 1984; Griffith, Mahy and Young 1986) in which we described their rituals, beliefs and form of service. In those early efforts, we sought to clarify mechanisms in the Church's meetings that individual members employed for psychologically helpful purposes. We also extended this work more recently to make clear what may have influenced transformation of this Barbados faith group from a marginalized, persecuted entity into an accepted denomination (Griffith, Mahy and Young 2008). We pointed out how the Church group, in becoming an accepted denomination, might then extend its influence and play a greater role in the broader society as a public health and social service agency. The earlier studies of the Barbados Spiritual Baptists have not examined the group's capacities to attract and hold its members, nor analysed fully ways in which the group may be therapeutic for its members. In addition, no extensive biographical exposition has been done, to my knowledge, of the Church's founder and continuing leader, Granville Williams. I intend, in this text, to focus on Archbishop Williams and the group, while presenting a coherent and comprehensive account that will both review earlier work and extend the inquiry into new arenas.

There is no doubt that the socioeconomic and political conditions that existed in the early part of the twentieth century in Trinidad are not the conditions now operative in the early part of the twenty-first century in Barbados. To a certain extent, the story of the Trinidad Spiritual Baptists, at least through the eyes of commentators like Lovelace (1983), is a narrative of liberation and freedom from colonial tyranny as much as it is also a story of the acquisition of individual and group self-esteem among Afro-West Indians. But Granville Williams was acquainted with the Trinidad context, at least as it was in the 1940s, and it is possible that, in participating in the struggle of Spiritual Baptists to liberate themselves from the tyranny of the colonial government in Trinidad, Williams sensed the opportunity to do something similar for his brothers and sisters in Barbados.

Understanding Williams's ideas is a prerequisite to grasping the meaning of the Church in the broader context of the Barbadian community, especially since he saw the need for transforming Barbadian society and its views on the access of black people to God's favours. I will describe the beliefs and rituals of the group, emphasizing the traditional Sunday and weekday services and other special activities such as "mourning", in addition to providing accounts of the Good Friday, baptismal and other key activities that occupy a significant place in the panoply of services carried on by this group throughout the Church's annual calendar.

I intend to clarify the factors that attract individuals to membership in the Church, as well as the elements that contribute to the retention of members. Dreams and visions play significant roles in the rituals and beliefs of this group, and they must be considered in the context of an explanatory framework for much of the group's doctrine. I will also point out distinctive architectural representations located within the precincts of the two existing Barbados Spiritual Baptist temples: Jerusalem Cathedral established in Ealing Grove, Christ

Figure 1.1 Jerusalem Apostolic Spiritual Baptist Cathedral. Ealing Grove, Christ Church, Barbados, c. 1982.

Figure 1.2 Jerusalem Apostolic Spiritual Baptist Cathedral. Ealing Grove, Christ Church, Barbados, 2009. (Photo by Felix Kerr.)

Figure 1.3 Zion Apostolic Spiritual Baptist Temple. Richmond Gap, St Michael, Barbados, 2008.

Church; and the smaller church called Zion Temple that is in Richmond Gap, just behind the wall of Westbury Cemetery in St Michael. These architectural renderings are a crucial part of the ritual secrecy that helps maintain the idea that members are a part of a special group. In turn, the group has knowledge of religious possibilities that colonial authorities kept hidden from them for many years.

The garments now worn by members of the Barbados group, unique and striking in appearance, bear symbols understood only by the initiated. These garments contribute to solidifying members' self-esteem, and they deserve to be described in detail. The organizational structure of the Church and the differentiated roles and functions of sub-groups within it are significant. These positions and activities contribute to the members' sense of ownership of what transpires within the organization and play a central role in cultivating their idea of belonging to something special. In the final chapter, I shall discuss the movement's future in Barbados, noting what I think are internal and external factors that may enhance or detract from stabilization of the Church and its potential to serve as both a religious organization and a social service system that might contribute effectively to the broader society's public health.

Similar to Jacobs (1996), in his work on Trinidad's Archbishop Griffith, I have had extended access to Granville Williams and have interviewed him many times, often for two and three hours at a stretch. I have also been a participant-observer of many Church services of the Barbados Spiritual Baptists during the past two and a half years, between 2007 and 2009. These contacts have been in addition to those that I have had with the Church in earlier years. I have also employed the qualitative approach of conducting numerous open-ended interviews with the intent of eliciting descriptions of first-person, subjective experiences from individual members of the Church and from others in the broader community who were not Church members.

I formally interviewed ten women and fifteen men who were members of the Church and seven men and women who were not Church members. But, in addition, I spoke to many members in informal conversations, as I tried to gain information about a Church practice or sought to find out who could be helpful in explaining a point to me. I used purposive sampling to determine whom I would interview formally. For example, knowing that I intended to explore the topic of Church garments, I sought out members who I expected could provide relevant information. When I learned of emerging conflicts in the Church, I tried to find members who would help me reach a fuller appreciation of both sides of the debate. I also conducted interviews of six clergy from other denominations so as to have reference individuals who could be helpful to me as I tried to grasp the theological import of what I learned about Spiritual Baptist doctrine. The non-members and the outside clergy enriched the cultural context for understanding the uniqueness of the Church in Barbados.

All of these conversations will be presented anonymously, except for the narrative interviews conducted with Archbishop Williams himself. I will often refer to these individuals as informants. Photographs utilized in the text and where individuals are identifiable are presented with permission of the subjects in those pictures. Additionally, photographs of the Churches and of Church members were taken with permission of Archbishop Williams, to whom I shall also refer as Leader, another term commonly used by Church members when they speak of their Archbishop. Throughout the text I will set out the meanings of rituals and symbols as they have been explained to me by informant members of the Church. But I will always present what has been confirmed by several members. This study was approved by the Human Investigation Committee of the Yale University School of Medicine.

I owe scholars who preceded me in studying Spiritual Baptist churches on other islands a debt of gratitude. I appreciate the information they provided and I have used it liberally to understand changes that Granville Williams made as he established his Church in Barbados. But these other scholars could not help me as I tried to fill in gaps about Williams's life. For example, try as I might, I could not learn much about his adolescent and young adult years. As the narrator of his own life story, Williams was reticent about that era in his life. And his own sister and others who knew him found it difficult to stray from the narrow story about the Church to talk about a past that is demonstrably less honorific than a present so full of Williams's declared accomplishments.

Throughout the text I will cite case examples from the lives of Spiritual Baptist members to illustrate key points in the narrative. These examples deserve consideration, as they are meant to ground my observations in reality and to demonstrate what members report as their own experiences within the context of the Spiritual Baptist Church. There is no attempt to claim that a particular member's view of life within the group is representative of what other members have experienced. Certainly, also, I do not intend any suggestion that one member's opinion should be seen as reflecting the views of a majority of members. The Spiritual Baptist faith (in addition to the tenets of qualitative methodology) precludes the facile drawing of conclusions from reports of any one member to be generalized to the rest of the group. This is so particularly because they claim that much Spiritual Baptist activity is a function of a member's interaction with the Holy Spirit, a phenomenon that is distinctively personal and unique. While observers will seek to find principles that may be drawn from descriptions that I will present, caution demands refraining from making assertions about the group based on what one member reports. Nevertheless, members' experiences still offer a window into the workings of the organization, a distinctive quality that is worth the effort at inquiry.

A curious phenomenon is now taking place, however, as public intellectuals such as Charles Johnson (2008) are now arguing that the experience of victimization may no longer be enough to make narratives of black people compelling and ultimately valuable. In the context of the Caribbean, Williams certainly came face-to-face with the relics of slavery and European colonization. But Barbados became an independent country in 1966 (Hoyos 1978), and some may therefore argue that, in viewing the narrative of the Barbados Spiritual Baptists, it is high time that the traditional Afro-Barbadian story rely on a different and modernized foundation. This is to say that the Afro-Barbadian narrative, to borrow language from the sociologist and historian Hilary Beckles (1998), could repose on a tableau of self-assertion and liberation. And instead of accentuating their history of colonial subservience, Barbadians could promote their own distinctive legitimacy in this novel and indigenous approach to religion. We shall see if this narrative transformation is possible, as we examine the stories of Granville Williams the individual and the Barbados Spiritual Baptists as a collective.

In any event, one thing is certain. The Spiritual Baptist faith and Granville Williams as one of its powerful symbols have both undergone a progressive metamorphosis over time. Neither one has stood still and watched the surrounding environment undergo an evolution without making some adaptation to what was being witnessed, as is reflected in the historic event that took place in Brooklyn, New York, on Saturday, 13 September 2008. On that occasion, Archbishop Granville Williams was elevated to membership in the Apostolic Patriarchate of the Spiritual Baptist faith. This group will now attempt to lead Spiritual Baptists all over the world in a unified structure that mirrors that of other traditional Christian groups. Williams will be the jurisdictional Patriarch for Barbados. Others were named to represent the jurisdictions of Trinidad and Tobago, Grenada, St Vincent and the Grenadines, and New York. The leader of the Patriarchate (His Excellency Dr Norris V. Ashton), called the Apostolic Patriarch of the Spiritual Baptist faith, will govern from New York City. Time will tell whether this effort to unify Spiritual Baptists will succeed.

Spiritual Baptists have been well known for their independence, both administratively and liturgically. Indeed, it is not clear whether the Spiritual Baptists who are migrants to Barbados from other islands like St Vincent will consider themselves subject to Patriarch Williams just because they have established churches in Barbados. On his return to the island from the service at which he was consecrated, the Vincentian Baptists participated in the celebrations and welcomed his return. But, of course, this is not quite the same as allowing Williams to set their church rituals or asking him to be the arbiter of member disputes within their organizations. Whatever the outcome of this effort to unify a leadership structure to govern these disparate religious subgroups that exist throughout the Caribbean and its attendant diaspora, Granville Williams has now been acknowledged as a leader of this international entity. This assures him a significant place in the history of the Spiritual Baptist movement in the Caribbean.

It should be obvious even from this brief introduction that Granville Williams has played a significant role in the founding and development of the Spiritual Baptist faith in Barbados. Hence, I have concentrated, to a large part in this text, on recounting the story of his life. This approach has resulted in a melding of biographical portraiture of Williams and psycho-cultural observations of the religious movement he founded. I have made an effort to highlight the voices of Williams, members of his congregation and other Barbadians who were both theologians and laypersons. But I acknowledge that in the narrative first-person style I adopted, my voice will be inevitably heard as I present how I probed and tested my own observations. Others will judge the value of this style. I believe it to be a useful approach in presenting work of this kind, a way of documenting my engagement with the project and articulating my service as a witness to the observations.

CHAPTER 2

The Cultural Context

IN HIS HISTORY OF Barbados, Hoyos (1978) points out that religious institutions, such as the Moravians and the Society for the Propagation of the Gospel, played a role in efforts to Christianize and educate the island's African slaves in the early 1700s. As the British proceeded to organize political and social structures on the island, the Anglican Church was a keen participant. The conceptual notion of parishes, into which Barbados was divided for purposes of administrative and political management, had the parish church's rector involved in the vestry, which was the name given to the entity that served as the local political leadership of each parish.

RELIGION

As the years progressed, other religious groups became well-known throughout Barbados, even though they may not have flourished to the same extent as the Anglicans, who enjoyed the status of being an endowed and established church on the island. The prestige and esteem of the Anglican Church were captured by Austin Clarke (2002) in his novel *The Polished Hoe*, which was set in early twentieth-century Barbados. The fictional St David's Anglican Church and its rector are landmark institutions in the narrative. Even London's famous St Martin in the Fields is touted in the novel as being the source of the BBC's radio broadcast of a Sunday church service heard in the island on its sole radio station. So the Anglican Church enjoyed standing as the premier religious institution in the cultural life of yesteryear's Barbados.

As a young boy in the 1940s, I realized that the Anglican Church was the church of the colonial government in Barbados. While a boy chorister in the island's St Michael's Cathedral choir, I recognized that we sang music in imitation of London's St Paul's Cathedral choir. There was no surprise among us choristers when, in celebration of Queen Elizabeth's 1953 coronation, we sang special anthems and watched men walking around in black "cutaway and tails" (that was our expression at the time for a man's formal daytime jacket, and we saw no redundancy in the expression) and grey striped pants, respecting the gravity of this thoroughly British moment.

The choir did not represent the full extent of my contact with religious groups, however. I went to morning Sunday school at the Moravian Church in Roebuck Street, and the afternoon saw me sitting quietly in classes at the nearby Bank Hall Methodist Church, the one just over the hill, as neighbours used to refer to it. I also knew that people from my Station Hill village in St Michael went to church regularly at Brother Tucker's Church, just down the road from the prison, before you reached the corner of Bank Hall and the Bridge Road. I do not recall any references being made to Tucker's church as belonging to a particular denomination. It was sufficient to know that his was not an Anglican, Methodist or Moravian edifice. Had it been so, his church would have been referred to with a peculiar formality that had developed around the names of churches from those denominations. Brother Tucker's church, situated on a slight embankment just above street level, was a geographic marker for those seeking clarity and specificity in a conversation. In other words, you could determine where a friend lived by asking whether his house was located above or below Tucker's house of worship.

I do not believe that there was anything unusual about this engagement with Brother Tucker, as I heard many people in my village refer to Sister Hawkins in the same way. Her church was a Bank Hall institution located on Holligan Road, and it was years before I detected any discussion of a denominational membership that could have defined Sister Hawkins and her organization. It was also telling that Sister Hawkins's church was a mere stone's throw from All Souls Anglican Church. But to all the people who lived in Bank Hall or frequently visited friends there, Sister Hawkins was as much a defining expression as All Souls. There was also no confusion in my mind when neighbours mentioned Sister Hardy, who had just returned from the United States and opened a church near the Bridge Road corner in St Michael. Once again, everybody knew that she was not a Moravian or a Methodist or an Anglican. But what she in fact was, denominationally speaking, never seemed at the time to be of concern to Barbadians.

Religious institutions played a central part in the lives of all my friends in that era. We all knew we had to respect Brother Tucker and Sisters Hawkins and Hardy in a quite formal way. We could never ignore anything they might say to us, and disrupting an open-air service they might be conducting in any community was understood to be an unpardonable sin. Sunday itself was a day of calm and repose. It was in those days not a time for frolicking or playing loud music. It did not mean that all the adults went to church, but a sense of careful deportment permeated the cultural air of the community and even those adults who did not go to church made some effort to make sure that their children went to Sunday school. Certainly by the 1950s, open-air services were well-established community events. Everybody I knew who lived in parishes close to Bridgetown was aware that on Sunday nights the Reverend Smith held court in the Bridgetown bus stand. That is where he conducted a service that attracted, at least for ten minutes or so, churchgoers who were exiting services from city churches that were located close to the bus stand.

It was at the time also a distinctive reality that most, if not all, schools marked the beginning of their day with morning prayers. In my elementary school, the headmaster conducted the ritual himself. There was always the reading of a lesson from the Bible. That is when we young boys heard expressions that eventually were engraved on our memories: "Go to the ant, thou sluggard; consider her ways and be wise" (Proverbs 6:6). The meaning of this biblical injunction was lost on most of us youngsters. But when linked to the other companion verse that always stuck in my mind – "How long wilt thou sleep, O sluggard?" (Proverbs 6:9) – I suspected that the headmaster was encouraging us to be diligent in our studies and in the yard work and house chores that most of us had to perform back at home. It was in these morning school rituals that we also became familiar with hymns like "Jerusalem the golden, with milk and honey blest"; "There is a green hill far away without a city wall, where the dear Lord was crucified who died to save us all". The repetition of these morning services enhanced our awareness of things religious, and the repetition continued throughout all the years at grammar school.

Indeed, by then we were attending compulsory classes of religious knowledge conducted by priests from the Anglican Church. Such classes were part of the day-to-day curriculum, and my uncertain memory tells me that only the one or two Catholic boys among us were exempt from the compulsory instruction.

In discussions with friends from my generation – that is to say, friends who were in elementary school in the 1940s and in grammar school in the 1950s – it was clear that we were all Protestants of one form or another. Several recalled that religion was even part of our childhood play. One friend reminded me that the ubiquitous church "procession" was a part of the play structure, and a broomstick was used as the crucifix. Children in these games also insisted on being the preacher in the make-believe service or on being the celebrant of the Holy Communion. When one lost the argument to be the leader of these ritual games, it was most unpleasant. One then had to decide whether to quit the game or continue in a decidedly less important role. Such was the presence of religion and church-related activity in the lives of youngsters at that time. These games allowed boys and girls to play together, and in spaces considerably less expansive than what was required for football or cricket.

It could therefore be safely said that during the first half of the twentieth century, when Barbados was a British colony, religion was an important and established part of the island's cultural fabric. The island was also distinctively Protestant, no doubt a function of its three-hundred-year-long colonial history. Still, the church groups were differentiated by their peculiar prestige in the community, with the Anglicans at the top of the list. There were, however, many other small faith groups, such as the ones already mentioned, that enjoyed local community standing and filled their congregations from people who lived in the regions surrounding the particular churches. The Catholics would expand their following later on, as individuals would come from the other islands that had undergone much greater French and Spanish influence than Barbados had ever experienced. No doubt, other factors would play a role in influencing the Catholic leadership to take a more visible position in the Barbados community and to enhance the standing of their denomination.

RELICS OF SLAVERY

We must remember that Barbados had been a slave community well into the first half of the nineteenth century. This would influence socio-political and economic factors in the island for years, to the point where present-day literary artists like Austin Clarke (2002) would contemplate the influence of slavery on the development of their key protagonists. Concepts of Obeah (commonly thought of as African-based religious beliefs involving sorcery) would appear in the language of Barbadians seeking to understand how the magic from African forefathers might have some role in what was transpiring on the present-day cultural scene. The sociologist Orlando Patterson (1967) performed an erudite analysis of Obeah as a derivative of slave beliefs specifically among the population in Jamaica. Morrow (1983) described it as a broader West Indian phenomenon with potential impact on health and pathology at the level of both the individual and the community. He noted its importation with the arrival of West African slaves in the Caribbean as early as the sixteenth century, and its flourishing despite the efforts of slave traders to control it.

At the local community level in Barbados, the term was still extant during my childhood. I recall how as boys we talked in hushed tones about "duppies", the spirits of the dead that could walk around and bring harm to the living, and about those who had more than a passing familiarity with those things. It was therefore no laughing matter one night when several of us boys had gone to urinate on graves located in the churchyard surrounding the church we were attending. This was a regular custom for us, as the line was too long in front of the latrine established for that purpose. Too many girls and women were there before us. Rather than go into church and suffer throughout the service, it made sense for us to duck behind the church and do what we had to do under cover of darkness. But when a duppy cried out, "Don't pee on me, don't pee on me", not one of us stayed around to verify whether the voice was real.

It was also a potent belief in our village that young men who went courting women should always be careful not to eat food prepared by these girlfriends. It was established, at least in the easily influenced minds of my buddies and me, that a woman could put things in the food she served that would turn a man "foolish" and have him proposing marriage long before it would have made practical sense to do so.

That was Obeah. It was Obeah, too, when a man, whom I knew well and who was at the end of his psychological rope in a family feud, decided to take things into his own hands. He was being tortured by his wife and daughters, with whom he was having a prolonged dispute. The women were amenable to settling things, but only on their terms. So the man sent a letter to them with distinctly noticeable oil marks on the edges of the envelope and perceptible evidence that salt had been placed on the oil. The resolution proceeded swiftly after that attempt at hexing, with the wife saying volubly that it was not necessary for him to have resorted to such un-Christian conduct. The woman was afraid and she let her friends know it. This response to suspected Obeah always puzzled me, and I thought that it was an overreaction of those who thought themselves the victims of its power. By that, I mean that my friends and I usually laughed at these stories.

However, it came quite close to home one day when my mother returned from a visit to someone's house and seemed visibly disturbed. The woman she had visited had lived among other non-Barbadian Caribbean people and was suspected of having a knowledge of religious matters that was distinct from that provided in the usual church settings. This was a gracious way of saying that the woman was suspected of dabbling in Obeah. As my mother told it, she arrived at the woman's house and was confronted by a collection of lighted candles burning in the middle of the day. In my mother's eyes, this was not the conventional time to be lighting candles. She instantly concluded that the woman was up to no good, and my mother took her leave precipitously. My mother's palpable fear troubled me, and I began to be more thoughtful about the place of Obeah in the lives of Barbadians living in the decades surrounding the Second World War. I am not suggesting that my mother, or even the man with his envelope stained by salt and oil, ever practised Obeah. But the man knew that his wife would be frightened by his manoeuvres, and my mother had no full confidence in her ability to ward off any spells. That was the reality in these people's lives at the time. I mention the presence of this Africanism in the secular life of Barbados to point out its coexistence with the well-established presence of religious institutions on the island. We shall also see the roles played by such elements in setting up the socio-cultural terrain that would characterize Barbados in the 1950s.

The previous existence of a slave community in Barbados, with black slaves and white slaveholders, also left as a persistently degrading relic the unequal social, political and economic relationship between blacks and whites on the island. It was a readily observable phenomenon, for example, that whites who were members of the St Michael's Cathedral congregation preferentially attended the 11 a.m. matins service. Few of them would be seen at the evening service. The island's cricket and football teams were easily characterized by the skin colour of their players. I do not suggest thereby that any team excluded players as a function of their skin colour. But I do know that certain teams would have surprised their fans had they turned up to play with a black player in their midst. C.L.R. James (1993) has described a similar state of affairs in Trinidad at the beginning of the twentieth century. The same habit of self-segregation, if not discrimination, was known to be practised by the Masonic lodges in Barbados. This practice was extended to the yacht club and the aquatic club all throughout my childhood and adolescent days. I recall clearly that there were watchmen placed strategically around those clubs to discourage boys like me from playing on the beaches of those institutions. I would not say that they operated with the force of law; however, they certainly did their best to make sure we understood that we did not belong there. We were not welcome. More to the point, of course, these black watchmen took their jobs seriously and spent considerable energy in pointing out that we were not a welcome sight on those beaches. These distinctions and differences were not, to my knowledge, written anywhere. They were just commonplace.

People in my village also spoke under their breaths about their beliefs that jobs at banks in town were distributed preferentially to whites and light-skinned blacks. Whether or not this was an employment custom that was carefully executed by white employers, it was a belief strongly held by those I kept company with. It was a notion discussed repeatedly, as people voiced the even broader view that establishments located in Bridgetown's Swan Street were more sympathetic towards hiring blacks than were those located in Broad Street, the principal thoroughfare of the business centre in town. The point was that some form of economic discrimination was believed to be operative. This was a prelude to the emergence of trade unions fighting for the economic rights of black people, those who had descended from the slave community on the island. In my interviews of some white Barbadians, it was their view that prestigious office jobs and bank positions were preferentially given to whites or to light-skinned blacks. As one of these individuals explained, white people were in control and they were protecting jobs for their own, a confirmation that the economic situation clearly favoured whites over blacks on the island.

The idea that there were differences between blacks and whites was further enhanced by the observation that many key posts on this small island were occupied by whites. The presence of a white Governor at Government House who represented Britain's monarch was a grim reminder of who we were as black people. And I never could get rid of the image of the Governor, with a distinctly patrician air, walking up the centre aisle of the Cathedral just before a service was to start. He would always be preceded by the Dean of the Cathedral and followed by his own aide-de-camp (ADC). The scene seemed perversely out of place to me in a ritual and at a time we were supposedly all equal in the sight of God. Of course, my complicated emotions and my childish analysis of race matters at that time did not allow me to think of the day when a black Governor General, accompanied by a black ADC, would be escorted up the aisle by a black Dean of the Cathedral. The business of equality in the sight of God was bound to take on increased complexity, although I wouldn't understand that until years later.

My puerile mind, for years, connected that tableau of the Governor and the Dean with the knowledge that some white people still paid rent for their seats in the Cathedral's pews. This renting of a church's seats meant, I was made to understand, that black people, who knew nothing about renting seats in a church, would have to get up if they were sitting in the seat at the time that the renter showed up for a service. It is true that I never saw that happen. But I would sit during sermon time in church and wonder what would happen if such an embarrassing situation ever occurred. I imagined that the sextons had worked out some diplomatic solution to resolve such an eventuality. But at other times I concluded, with no evidence at all to buttress my belief, that white people had colluded to avoid such public conflict by attending primarily the matins service that was not generally popular with blacks. All of these ideas were the reflections of a black adolescent in the Barbados of the 1950s. As a friend recently said to me while we both laughed at our thoughts of over fifty years ago, we had no proof of the racial backgrounds of the people whose names were inscribed on the pews. Some of them may have been black renters, for all we knew at the time, although we certainly did not think so then.

The social separation of blacks and whites also existed in ways that were not always obvious to the casual observer. Educational facilities in Barbados were not segregated, and distinguished schools like Harrison College and Queen's College had their students from all ethnic and socio-economic backgrounds sitting in the same classrooms. What these students did after school was often a different matter. Some continued to mix as they played table tennis together or went to the beach together. But my white friends stated that cross-racial dating was not encouraged by parents, and white adolescent women who had serious black boyfriends were usually the cause of noisy disagreements inside their families. Such relationships did not usually proceed to marriage. In one that did go that way, however, the arrival of the baby from the racially mixed relationship was greeted by the child's white family members' exclaiming that the baby had a "lick of the tar brush". As the mother explained to me, one could take the comment as a bad joke or be angered by it. But there was no misapprehending the white family's point of view concerning the racially mixed relationship. The baby's mother knew that her own father had drawn the line at marrying outside the race.

EMERGENCE OF THE SPIRITUAL BAPTISTS

It was to this Barbadian cultural context that thirty-four-year-old Granville Williams, a Spiritual Baptist preacher and a Barbadian by birth, returned in 1957 from living in Trinidad. He had been residing there since 1944, and after joining that religious faith had opened his own church in the St Ann's section of Port of Spain. But he had decided to return to his native land of Barbados and preach the gospel in a country that had not previously heard the doctrine of the Spiritual Baptists. The Reverend Mr Williams established the first Spiritual Baptist Church in Barbados and has continued to oversee his group's development since its inception. Since his return, however, other autonomous Spiritual Baptist groups have been formed on the island. Their leaders are reportedly, for the most part, immigrants from the island of St Vincent and they will not be a part of this story of the Barbados Spiritual Baptists. The Vincentian Baptists, however, apparently attend certain special services at Williams's church from time to time, and they acknowledge Williams's accomplishments and his leadership in building the Spiritual Baptist faith so successfully in Barbados. In addition to the churches led by immigrants from other islands, it is acknowledged that an occasional disgruntled Barbadian has left Williams's Church and attempted to set up a new congregation. Such initiatives seem to have petered out or have remained so small as to be without much impact on the local scene of Spiritual Baptist developments. Of course, this state of affairs may change in the future.

The Spiritual Baptist movement has been present in other Caribbean islands, particularly in Trinidad (where they were originally referred to as Shouter Baptists) and St Vincent (where they were called Shakers), from about the late nineteenth century. The movement in those islands has had considerable visibility over the years, but has only gained prestige and recognition relatively recently. The group was outlawed in St Vincent in 1912. Then, a few years later in 1917, Trinidad authorities moved to have Spiritual Baptist meetings declared illegal. In his elegant and moving review of the movement in Trinidad, Jacobs (1996) traces the history of this persecution and even describes a few of the court cases that were brought against Shouters for keeping their services. The court actions also suggest that the police regularly broke up Shouter meetings before the Prohibition Ordinance had been passed. Jacobs (1996) points out that one such illegal disruption of a service by the police led to their being sued in court. The resulting decision was favourable to the Shouter Baptist plaintiff.

Criticism of the Spiritual Baptists in Trinidad centred on their being a noise nuisance, as their services employed ringing of hand bells, falling in the Spirit, and loud singing and dancing. But there were also hints about their engaging in other, more immoral practices. These unspecified allusions appeared to target the Spiritual Baptist practice of "mourning", which I will later describe at considerable length. This persecution of the Shouter Baptists did not go unnoticed. In 1931, for example, the Trinidad publication known as the *Beacon* published an editorial lambasting the Prohibition Ordinance (Editorial Notes 1931). The *Beacon* was published at the time by Albert Gomes and colleagues, who were well known for their anti-establishment political views. Gomes went on to make a political alliance around 1946 with the Spiritual Baptists, who worked tirelessly to have him elected to the legislature. In turn, he kept their grievances alive and agitated to have the Prohibition Ordinance overturned. The repeal of the Trinidad statute finally occurred in 1951; the 1912 St Vincent ordinance was overturned in 1965 (Henney 1982).

When Granville Williams arrived in Trinidad in 1944, it was a time of upheaval for the Spiritual Baptists on that island, given that their status as an outlawed religious group seemed to have been clearly recognized. Indeed, this period of religious persecution in Trinidad has been immortalized by Earl Lovelace in his novel *The Wine of Astonishment* (1983). When Granville Williams decided to join the faith in 1945, the Spiritual Baptist Leader who baptized him was Elton George Griffith (no relation to this author), who went on to become an Archbishop in the movement and was in fact the head of the political group that sought to overturn the Prohibition Ordinance. According to Williams, it was also Griffith who was the leading architect of the successful political alliance with Albert Gomes. Williams, too, had had the services of his own fledgling church disrupted by the police during his first years in Trinidad. Consequently, he was aware of what it meant to be part of a faith group that was considered to be outside the law by the country's government. This experience with formal persecution and informal resistance to his religious beliefs would serve him well during the early phase of his return to Barbados.

In discussing the Spiritual Baptists of the Caribbean, the question naturally emerges about their origin. I have seen no definitive text that clearly dates their first appearance in any community. Jacobs (1996) concentrates on elucidating the history of the movement in Trinidad and he seems to suggest that traces of the movement began to appear in Trinidad with the migration of black American ex-slaves to the island around 1815. These black former soldiers had apparently fought on the side of the British against the Americans in the War of 1812, and their reward was to receive their freedom and to be resettled in Trinidad. These "merikun Baptists" apparently followed Baptist liturgy, although they quickly introduced other unique and indigenous practices into their worship services, some of which caused criticism from English Baptist ministers. It appears that the black Americans maintained their rituals, and the Spiritual Baptist movement gradually developed and grew stronger. Henney's observations (1982) in St Vincent suggest that the Shakers were functioning on that island in the late nineteenth century. Certainly, given that they were outlawed by 1912, they must have been a significant nuisance to the authorities around the turn of the century. Neither of these historical strands, however, explains whether there was any solid connection between the movements in Trinidad and St Vincent and how those connections may have been established. Migration of church members is a possible explanation, although no one seems sure of that. In my discussion of this matter with Jacobs, he suggested that while several companies of the American ex-slaves went to Trinidad, one of them may have gone to St Vincent. Migration of Spiritual Baptists explains the appearance of Granville Williams in Barbados; the cropping up of several Vincentian groups in Barbados; and the emergence of Spiritual Baptist churches in New York, Toronto, Boston and other venues.

In 1974, Dr Cuthbert Joseph (Trinidad's parliamentary representative for Port of Spain East) gave a speech to mark the laying of the Foundation Stone and blessing of St Peter's Spiritual Baptist Cathedral in Gonzales, Port of Spain (Joseph 1974). In that address, Joseph theorized that the Spiritual Baptist faith was transplanted into Trinidad directly from the Yoruba tribe in West Africa. He argued that Trinidad was one of the Caribbean colonies that received Yoruba slaves after the 1833 abolition of slavery. This explained what he saw as the connection between the Aladura religion of the Yorubas and the Spiritual Baptist religion of the Caribbean. Using his 1939 observations of the Trinidad Spiritual Baptists, Herskovits (1978) has interpreted much of what he has seen as clear African influence in the rituals of the Spiritual Baptists. As we shall see later, the emergence of Spiritual Baptist ritual has not been a static affair. Rather, the development of the movement appears to have been a syncretistic phenomenon, with aspects of their rituals coming from different sources. Laitinen (2002) has added to this debate, however, by pointing out that syncretism does not account for the continuous transformation observed in the Spiritual Baptist religion. In other words, the mixture of African and Christian features does not alone explain the richness of Spiritual Baptist rituals. The richness comes also from creolization, which is a process of invention and creativity that arises from the confluence of a structured system and individual experiences such as those gained in mourning. Taylor (2001) has pointed out that other scholars prefer the term symbiosis, which suggests the spatial juxtaposition of cultural influences without the fusing of one with the other.

In this brief review, I have set out to remind readers that religious institutions have played significant roles in the lives of Barbadian citizens. I have done so through resorting to established scholarship, but also by relying on my own memories and those of Barbadian informants who could recall their experiences over the last fifty or sixty years. I have tried to bring to life the cultural context of Barbados around 1957 when Granville Williams became the first Spiritual Baptist preacher to take up the challenge of introducing for the first time this faith to a conservative religious population on the island. In addition, I have drawn attention to other, broader forces that would emerge in the years leading to the dawn of the twenty-first century.

Chatfield (1998) has also provided us another type of framework that might be useful in examining this narrative of the Barbados Spiritual Baptists. He saw the Caribbean Spiritual Baptists as similar to the movement of independent churches in Africa, a movement that has steadily eroded the influence of what he calls the mission-founded churches (those dominated by the white colonizers) on that continent. Chatfield therefore considers the Spiritual Baptists as an example of African independency in the Caribbean and notes their potential significance as "vehicles for the introduction or re-incorporation of elements of African spirituality, for the empowerment of women, as protest against white or missionary domination of the churches, and in some limited cases as agents of political pressure against colonization" (95). His argument articulates another vantage point for viewing Williams's contributions.

CHAPTER 3

Granville Williams

The Early Years

GRANVILLE WILLIAMS WAS BORN in Barbados on 3 October 1923 in an area of Christ Church parish known as Rollins that was near to St Christopher's Anglican Church. He was the sixth of seven children born to Eldica and Seifort Callender. The first five children apparently died young, as Granville Williams never knew any of his older siblings. But he did grow up with his younger sister, Esme, who later became a Bailey through marriage. She is now one of the senior Abbesses in the Spiritual Baptist organization. It remains unclear why baby Granville was christened a Williams instead of a Callender. Apparently his maternal grandfather was a Williams and a soldier whose name was much admired by someone in the family. It is puzzling why that family name was put on the birth certificate. Similarly, little is known about the early deaths of his older siblings. In his childhood years, his parents owned a small grocery shop. His father also reportedly spent much of his time taking care of large parcels of land that he had inherited from his own father. Some of that land is the terrain on which presently stands the Spiritual Baptist Cathedral, located in what is now called Ealing Grove, Christ Church. At some time, the father was also involved in building fishing boats.

Young Granville Williams did not have the time necessary for developing a sustained and mature relationship with his father. Eldica and Seifort Callender apparently had a significant quarrel that led to Mr Callender's decision to leave Barbados (and his wife and two children) and settle in Trinidad.

Granville was about nine years old at the time, and Esme was about five. This explains Mother Bailey's statement that she didn't know much about her father during those early years. She got to know him only after he returned to Barbados from Trinidad. The Archbishop, however, can recall his father's wish that his son be a judge, and he can still hear his father's voice advising him to study so that he would eventually "sit on the bench". The origin of such a dream for his son is hard to fathom, as a black man sitting as a judge in 1930s Barbados would have been a difficult tableau for any young non-white boy to visualize. But this father, who in his son's eyes was strict, possibly thought that these views could be implemented because of his extensive land holdings. The father may also have been setting his plan into action when, in addition to sending his son to elementary school at St Christopher's, he made sure that young Granville received extra school instruction at home – a privilege that Barbadians of a certain economic means often offered their children. They called it "going to lessons" or "getting lessons from a school teacher". Boosting the usual educational offerings was a way of improving the chances of a child's eventual success in life. Mr Callender's hopes for his son may have been summed up in his expressed wish that Granville develop the habit of associating with upper-class people.

His father's departure for Trinidad, however, left Granville and Esme in the exclusive care of Eldica Callender, who promptly moved her family to Black Rock, St Michael. She enrolled her two children in St Stephen's elementary school and continued Granville's after-school private tuition. She also maintained the strictness that had surrounded Granville and Esme. Other parents had to beg her to let Granville come out to play with their children. I found it unusual to learn that, growing up, Granville had not pitched marbles or played hopping-ball cricket with neighbourhood friends. As he described it, he went from home to school and then back home. Such a parental attitude towards a child would have been unforgivable in my boyhood village, where parents believed that a boy had to learn from receiving "hard knocks" in his life. Some of those disappointments were expected to come from neighbourhood sporting activities.

Eldica Callender possibly had her own ideas about being protective of her only "boy-child", a term that Barbadians invented to make clear their possessiveness of male children. Her need to surround Granville with her own version of a cocoon may have been partly nurtured by her being abandoned by a husband who went off to Trinidad. Granville did not go on to secondary school. He completed seventh standard at St Stephen's (in those days, one reached seventh standard around age thirteen) and then remained unemployed and apparently without direction throughout his teenage years. About age seventeen, he tried to become a boxer. In his words, his mother stopped him before he even started. She showed up the night of his very first fight and had him return home with her, without the exchange of a single punch between him and his opponent. Whether she entreated him to return home or simply issued instructions that he do so is unclear. But he said that it was also she who nixed his idea of becoming a seaman. Just before leaving on a ship to Curaçao, he went to say good-bye to her and tell her that he had signed up, without her permission, to make the voyage. But she was afraid of the war that was going on about that time, and he obeyed her and stayed home. He then went to join the local police force. She withheld her permission there, too, and he never wore the police uniform. Some time during those years, Granville's father wrote and encouraged him to join him in Trinidad. But Mrs Callender did not support that idea either. At least, she did not support it at first. Her opinion was that her husband was in Trinidad living with another woman. Her resentment did not allow her to be so forgiving as to encourage her son to go live with her estranged husband in that island that so simultaneously repelled and attracted Barbadians. Things changed when her husband returned to live in Barbados in the early 1940s. This time, when Granville's father encouraged him to try his luck in Trinidad, his mother agreed. She also partly changed her mind because she thought that a distant cousin whom she liked was then living in Trinidad. And so, 1944 saw twenty-one-year-old Granville Williams go off to Trinidad to find his fortune. It was the initial excursion of a young man who had been, to that point, protected and coddled zealously by his mother, and abandoned in his key formative years by his father.

Granville Williams was born a few years before the world depression of 1929 that had provoked a worsening in the economic condition of the West Indies (Hoyos 1978, 201). For a while, the sugar industry rebounded, but by the mid-1930s the situation had deteriorated again. As Hoyos points out, by 1937 the sugar industry was restricted, with a reduction in the number of people it employed (202). The local Barbadian population continued to rise, which caused considerable strain on the economic infrastructure of the island. In Barbados, conditions were exacerbated by the foreclosure of employment possibilities usually offered by emigration. It is unclear how the economic conditions affected Seifort Callender personally when he left for Trinidad in 1932 or 1933. We do not know whether the struggle between him and his wife was more of a factor in his decision than was the economic situation of the day.

Granville Williams would have been a young boy of fourteen or so when the crowds met in Bridgetown on the evening of 26 July 1937 to protest the deportation of Clement Payne, who had apparently been holding public meetings and preaching "the gospel of trade unionism" (Hoyos 1978, 208). The authorities were obviously worried by the public's interest in Payne's ideas, and they saw fit to remove him from the island. But this act ignited a broad public disturbance that led to the death of about fourteen people and injuries to another fifty citizens (208). The official commission that investigated the cause of the riot concluded that Payne's deportation had only been the spark that ignited things. The unrest had been there for some time and was obviously linked to the harsh realities of the economic situation on the island (208). This was the context in which Granville Williams and his younger sister were raised by a single mother. They were, of course, too young at the time to appreciate the implications of the political and economic unrest. Decades would pass before the average Barbadian would understand the meaning of the 1930s for the Caribbean.

THE TRINIDAD YEARS (1944–1957)

As mentioned before, it was 1944 when twenty-one-year-old Granville Williams went off to make a new life in Trinidad. He was following a path that had been travelled by earlier generations of Barbadians who had gone to Cuba, Guyana, Panama, England, Canada and the United States. Migration to foreign lands had long been established as a means of contending with the lack of employment opportunity at home. Even though his mother's encouragement was muted, his father had continued to tell him that this trans-island move was worth trying. His father had also left a house in Trinidad that his son could use, and it was there that young Granville went to reside. As he recounted, people living in the house were not very pleased to see him, since they believed that he had been sent to get them out of the house so that it could be sold. His arrival therefore created a certain tension in the Gonzales neighbourhood where the home was located.

Granville's disagreements with people who had their own interest in his father's property took a turn for the worse one evening when he was returning home from a christening he had attended in an area called Mova. As he approached his house on a bicycle that he had borrowed from a friend, he saw a wheel of fire spinning in front of him. A voice spoke to him and said, "You are lucky. You have on your only suit." In retrospect, he has often wondered whether this encounter with a disembodied voice marked his entry into spirituality. When he did arrive at the house, he realized that someone had made an effort to burn it down. His arrival prevented total destruction of his home, however. He also recognized that it was good that he had left the christening service before its conclusion. His early departure for home had been occasioned by a non-specific feeling of malaise that had just inexplicably come over him. In the Caribbean of that day, such unexplained phenomena that resulted in benefits to people were often eventually interpreted in religious terms. In addition, the appearance of the wheel, this universally recognized Old Testament symbol, would take on greater psychological significance later in Williams's life: it would be recognized by Williams as an important symbol in the Spiritual Baptist movement.

This encounter with the fire was a concrete manifestation of the animosity displayed towards him in light of the collective conclusion that he was his father's heir to the house. People wanted him gone. In his view, some even wanted him dead. While he would not turn tail and run, he began to think about living elsewhere. One day while he was at home reading, he heard someone call his name. He looked around, but there was no one in sight.

Then the voice asked three times, "You want a house?"

He replied, "Yes."

The voice's rejoinder was, "I'll give you a house."

Williams was apparently disturbed by this exchange and the absence of a concrete source for the voice. A little upset, he locked his door and left the house, not knowing what to expect. But he soon met a friend who was on the way to visit him. The man told him, "I bring something for you," and handed him a key. It represented the offer of a new residence. Williams moved into this residence that was located in St Ann's and bought some furniture for his new lodging. He was pleased to move away from Gonzales and all the interpersonal acrimony engendered by the struggles over his father's house. He liked his salesman job at the nearby Coca-Cola factory, and things were beginning to look up. He also began to take note of a new pattern in his life: every time he encountered a significant problem, a solution would crop up and the stress would be lifted off his shoulders. It was almost as though someone were looking out for him. For example, he would run out of money; then, almost miraculously, money would turn up from some unlikely source. The problem with his residence had been a similar matter. In the midst of his quandary, a friend appeared with a key to a new place for him to live. With this good fortune constantly shadowing him, he began to display a new attitude of thankfulness towards God, while recognizing that suffering and persecution would be a constant part of his life.

As Williams was reading his Bible one evening, he turned to Acts 8, which describes the encounter between Philip and the Ethiopian eunuch. The passage haunted him, and he went to discuss its meaning with a friend, mirroring the eunuch's own concern that he may not have understood clearly the scripture that he had been reading about the prophet Isaiah. Williams's friend told him that the passage meant that he was being given a sign that he had an obligation to serve God. And once again, reflecting the story of Philip and the eunuch, Williams set about to find someone who could baptize him and put him on the path of righteousness. A friend took him to see a Spiritual Baptist minister, and he first went to church on a Wednesday night. He recalled being met at the entrance to the church by two young ladies, who took him directly to the altar to pray. His baptism was scheduled for the following Sunday, and he attended the tarrying service that was usually held in those days on the Saturday night before the baptism. In these services, Church members and candidates for baptism would sing and pray all night.

On Sunday morning, Williams was taken to the beach for the baptismal service, and a white cloth band was placed over his eyes. His first clear experience of having a vision then began to unfold. He saw the Lord Jesus descending stairs from heaven and looking at him. John the Baptist was also there with a basin. Jesus poured something into the basin, and John emptied the basin's contents into the sea, which began to boil. Williams said that he fainted at that point, which prompted a nurse from the congregation to ask him, once he'd recovered, whether he was sick and wanted to postpone the baptism. He insisted on going through with it. Williams kept the vision to himself, but no doubt saw it as confirmation that his own baptism was itself a wonderful event and his entrance into the spiritual life was being heralded by Jesus himself. In addition, since visions were important in the world of the Spiritual Baptists, this was evidence that he was well on his way in his new life, marked as it was by this auspicious beginning.

Williams's baptism was conducted by Leader Elton George Griffith, who thereby became his spiritual father – a relationship in the Spiritual Baptist orthodoxy that is, from its inception, an immutable connection. Many Spiritual Baptists see this relationship as superior to the link created by what they call a carnal father-child relationship. Williams also recounted another vision linked to his baptism. He saw an army of people coming towards him dressed all in white robes. They set up a queue that passed through a little hut. His turn came to enter the hut. When he got inside, he was surprised by the vast size of the interior. There were four men inside, one of whom wrote Williams's name with an enormous pen.

> Williams asked, "How do you know my name? I saw you write my name."
>
> One man replied, "We know your name."
>
> "Who are you?"
>
> At this, the men laughed and said, "You know us."
>
> "No, I don't."
>
> "I am the Archangel Michael." The others added that they were Raphael, Uriel and Gabriel, all archangels.
>
> "What is the name of this place?"
>
> "This is the Registry."
>
> "For what?"
>
> "For everyone who has been baptized. We were at your baptism. Tell us what you saw when you fainted on the beach."
>
> "You know a lot. What I saw is my business."
>
> The archangels laughed again, no doubt at the arrogance of Williams's reply, and one of them said, "We were there."
>
> To that he answered, "Why didn't I see you?"
>
> "You couldn't see us. The Lord is waiting to meet you in Jerusalem."

Williams explained that, at the end of this dialogue, he found himself on the way to Jerusalem. The vision ended there. He saw in it the commencement of his spiritual education.

It takes time for any observer to appreciate fully all that visions can mean to Spiritual Baptist initiates. It is also not easy for outsiders to grasp the authenticity of the revelations. Indeed, much of the time, it seems pointless to worry about trying to verify the authenticity, although I point out later that Spiritual Baptists don't always accept what they hear from one another. But in this particular case, we have Granville Williams confirming that his baptism was real. Through this ceremonial act of rebirth and redemption, he had his name inscribed in the books located in the Registry. Furthermore, he was in contact with archangels and was set on the way to Jerusalem to see the Master. The highlight of his visions is that Jesus and John the Baptist were at his baptism and did things for him that not even the archangels knew about. This detail reconfirmed his sense of uniqueness, a fundamental aspect of the Spiritual Baptist experience with visions and dreams. This singularity, this notion that he is a specially selected individual and one who is formally blessed, is an integral part of how he sees himself. He thinks it all started when he was a boy and neighbours thought that he was "out of the ordinary". So if someone had a special trip to make, such as going to see a lawyer, little Granville was invited as a companion who was expected to bring good fortune to the adult. I shall return later to this aspect of exceptionality that is a fundamental dimension of Williams's definition of self.

As is often the case with Spiritual Baptist members who are assiduous in their devotion to their temple, Granville Williams fell in love with a woman who attended his home church in St Ann's. Eurise John was a Tobagonian who had been raised in Trinidad. She apparently was the centre of attention from several suitors. But he won her heart, and they were married in 1946, at an Anglican church since the Spiritual Baptist churches did not have the legal authority to preside over marriages. They had three children, who all presently live in Trinidad. Ms John died in 1988, but she and her husband had been estranged since the late 1950s.

The time eventually came when Williams felt called to establish his own church. He apparently did so in 1947 or 1948 with the blessing of his spiritual father, and he went on to build a significant following throughout Port of Spain. His decision to make the move was, of course, validated through dreams and visions that urged him to set up his own church. Despite this move to assert his own independence, he speaks proudly of having served as Elton Griffith's deputy on many occasions. It was with Griffith that he participated in supporting the political aspirations of Albert Gomes. It was also the time when he became thoroughly familiar with the social claims being made against the Spiritual Baptist movement. From time to time he would be called to attend a hearing at one police station or another and to answer questions about the illegal religious movement to which he belonged. In Parliament, reference was repeatedly made to the Spiritual Baptists as a noisy group and one that regularly created disturbances. It was claimed that when they "got in the spirit" at night, those living in houses adjoining the Spiritual Baptist temples could hardly sleep. Furthermore, members of the group were said to have bad habits: for example, they stole neighbours' poultry. And it was common to make allusions to the lewd sexual practices that accompanied the mourning ritual of the Spiritual Baptists.

It is evident from Williams's accounts that his stay in Trinidad was a period of considerable maturing. Far away from his parents and his sister, he developed his own unique support system that seemed intricately linked to his experiences in the Spiritual Baptist faith. In a relatively short period of time, he reportedly developed a reputation as an impressive Leader of his own congregation and as someone who knew well the doctrine of the movement. Trinidad's society was also very complicated in matters of religion, given that there were Spiritual Baptists who also practised Shango rituals that were founded on beliefs in pan-African deities. Ward (1979–1980) points out that the Trinidadian Shango cult emerged as a syncretic religion-based mixture of African Yoruba tradition and Catholic practices. Consequently, there were constant competitions among Spiritual Baptist Leaders to prove who was authentically Christian and also most knowledgeable about the theoretical aspects of their religion and adept at handling the practical rituals of their faith. In such competitions, Leader Granville apparently handled himself well, which burnished his reputation among Trinidadians far and wide. Jacobs (1996) has effectively described the transformation of the Trinidad movement from a prohibited cult to an accepted religious movement. And Henry (2008) has pointedly articulated the conclusion that both the Spiritual Baptist faith and the Orisha (Shango) faith in Trinidad have undergone socio-political legitimization, thereby enjoying present-day standing in the broader society, as was unexpected during Williams's stay in Trinidad.

Williams wanted to build up a reputation for fearlessness in the face of the legal prohibition against Spiritual Baptist meetings. He took pride in recounting that, at a baptismal service one Sunday morning, the police showed up shouting their intent to arrest everybody. Most people ran. But Williams stood his ground, especially as he could hardly leave his nine candidates for baptism who had their eyes banded. They couldn't see to leave the scene, and Williams felt he had an obligation to stay and protect his charges. He held his ground and had a conversation with the sergeant in charge. The policeman was persuaded by Williams to leave the group in peace. They shook hands, and he continued his worship.

At another service he was leading, a police inspector and two constables showed up. Williams began to preach, and his words so impressed the inspector that the officer soon fell to the ground, apparently overcome by emotion. The constables took away the inspector, who returned at a later date to visit Williams and speak about how the preacher's words had affected him. The inspector gave testimony one night in the church about Williams's effect on him and he promised thereafter to protect Williams from any further police disruption of his services. Of course, this episode serves as further proof of Williams's testimony to his own exceptionality.

Williams described the way in which Spiritual Baptist members and Leaders would compete against each other by "proving" one another – the unique Spiritual Baptist way of verifying whether a person's spiritual credentials are authentic. As he explained it, a Leader from one church might, for example, accept an invitation to make a pilgrimage and visit another church. The host church's Leader could then surprise the invited Leader and members by writing Spiritual Baptist seals in chalk all over the road leading to the host church. (We shall discuss the importance of seals and symbols at considerable length later on. For the present, a seal commonly used by Spiritual Baptists is the intersecting square and compass made familiar by Freemasonry.) In this instance, the seals could be interpreted either as an effort to encompass the pilgrimage in spirituality and holiness, or as an act of minor malice intended at least to frighten the visitors and cause some disarray in their ranks. At a minimum, the visiting Leader needs to assert leadership, calm down all his members and write his own seals on the road with the unstated confidence that he knows what steps to take to protect his church members. In effect, he has to demonstrate that he possesses the requisite theoretical knowledge to combat whatever traps are being set for him, as well as the artistic confidence to act with grace and aplomb as he goes about his own rituals. In anticipation of such encounters, a visiting Leader might actually avoid this kind of confrontation by bringing along a Leader from another congregation who is well versed in these rituals and stylistically suited to compete in this public way. It is said that such encounters were anticipated and enjoyed by Spiritual Baptists all over Trinidad. Onlookers would come from far and wide to witness these spiritual confrontations. The theatre provided by these interactions lent itself to dissemination by word of mouth, even though it is likely that many individuals did not understand the full import of what they were viewing. In his own words, Granville Williams enjoyed these matters, and the confidence displayed through his public persona magnified his charisma in the eyes of Trinidadian onlookers.

In this regard, one could ask why pastors should be expected to be different from professionals in any other discipline. Most people bring a certain confidence to their professional activity and take pleasure in the respect offered by their peers and those they serve. Spiritual Baptist Leaders enjoy this esteem that flows to them from their members. But they are not protected from spiritual inquiries or doubts emanating from outsiders. From several informants I heard the story about a visiting Leader who attended a church service in Barbados. At that service, members of the congregation tested the Leader about the authenticity of the regalia and vestments he was wearing. This Leader was challenged to explain the spiritual origin and meaning of his garments. In the eyes of those present at this "proving", the Leader did not effectively provide an explanation of his spiritual uniform, which he was forced to remove in full view of all those present. As the story goes, he only got back his vestments after praying and undergoing some period of re-education. Such stories are naturally complex. It is not evident what prompted the attack on the visiting Leader. Perhaps he appeared unduly humble and vulnerable. Or, those who instigated the proving may have been confident they could win their confrontation because they had the advantage of being in their home church. My informants also agreed that no one they knew would dare to take on Granville Williams in such a public spectacle. He is seen as too confident, too knowledgeable, too in tune with the Holy Spirit to be ambushed in a proving session conducted by average church members.

Granville Williams had left Barbados in 1944 without a clearly defined strategic plan for his future. He did have some expectation that things would fall into place through his following the footsteps of his father, who had gained a respectable reputation in Trinidad. So a number of people were helpful to Williams because they had known and liked his father. Williams had a place to live and he kept his job at the Coca-Cola Company during the time he was there. Once he became a Spiritual Baptist through baptism by immersion, his social contacts expanded and he was transformed by his new commitment to a special religious life. At the side of Elton George Griffith, his spiritual father, Williams learned about the unique political and economic context of the Caribbean and Trinidad. I have already mentioned Griffith's connection to Albert Gomes and this politician's struggle for the black underclass in Trinidad. It was also Griffith and Gomes who mapped the strategy for having the Spiritual Baptist Prohibition repealed in 1951. These experiences with Griffith and Gomes also led Williams to be on Gomes's political platforms throughout Trinidad during election time.

Williams has reported that he learned other things from Griffith as well. In one instance, the two men were together when police arrested Griffith on a charge of having raped a girl. Williams explained that the charge was dropped once doctors verified that the girl was still a virgin. It was the girl's grandmother who had apparently instigated the trumped-up claims. She had encouraged the complaint from the adolescent girl, allegedly because her own advances had been rejected by Griffith. It was therefore arguably the case of a spurned woman's being hostile to the man she wanted. As it turned out, the police were reported to have pursued a complaint against the woman for having made a false report. But it was Griffith who intervened to have the charges against the woman dropped. Williams explained that he admired Griffith's capacity for forgiveness in this matter. Later on, Griffith's Christian spirit revealed itself once again when he asked Williams to accompany him, as they had to go pray for this same woman. She had fallen on hard times and needed prayers. While Williams complied with this request from his spiritual father, he conceded in our discussions that, at the time, he was not possessed of enough humility and patience to react calmly to the treatment the woman had meted out to Griffith. Williams was not sorry for her, even in the midst of her suffering. As for praying on her behalf, he described himself as kneeling down, but unable to offer up even the simplest intercessory request for the woman. His youth and spiritual inexperience got in the way of his pastoral duty. His headstrong personality would not let him empathize with the woman. He still had much to learn about life and religion and that, in common Barbadian parlance, what had missed him hadn't necessarily passed him yet.

PREPARING FOR BARBADOS

Nevertheless, he was getting ready. He was preparing himself for the day he would strike out on his own. Setting up his own church in St Ann's was the preliminary step that preceded his major decision to return to Barbados. When that time came in 1957, he had already had a number of visions confirming his call to take the word of God to the island of Barbados. In one such vision, an angel took him to the Lord Jesus, who anointed him with oil and blessed him. Jesus told him that he was sent to preach the gospel throughout the world and that he would heal all manner of sickness and would work miracles. Jesus also told him that he would even raise the dead. To this, Williams reacted with disbelief and said, "Lord, tell me what to do to raise the dead." Jesus replied, "Just wait for the manifestation of the Spirit." Williams then thanked Him and walked away.

The influence of this type of vision resides partly in its power to help resolve a matter that could lead to a significant transformation of a person's life. But the vision also consecrates the sacredness of a relationship between God and the person having the vision at the same time that the person is called to carry out a specific act. There is therefore simultaneous confirmation of the vocational act as the individual is selected as unique and special in the eyes of God.

Williams's decision to leave for Barbados could not have been an easy one, even if it was reinforced and confirmed by the Spirit in several visions. He was not an independently wealthy man, although he had the option of living with his mother, who was still alive. His father or his father's estate may have provided some measure of support for him. But he also had a wife and three children to feed, and there could be no assurance that he would find supporters in Barbados just waiting for his arrival so that they could be converted to this religion that was new to the Barbadian psyche. Strange as it may seem, Williams's Trinidadian church members did not know of his plans to settle permanently in Barbados. Perhaps he avoided telling them so as to permit an easy return to Trinidad if things didn't go well. He explained that his plan was to have his wife direct the church in Trinidad while he set about his work as a missionary to the people in Barbados. But within months of his arrival in Barbados, his wife arrived with the children in tow. She stayed about three weeks before their relationship became so estranged that she took the children and returned to Trinidad. He reported that, after her arrival in Barbados, the Com-

Figure 3.1 Leader Granville Williams (c. 1955) before his return to Barbados from Trinidad. In his hand is his pessy. (Taken from the Church's programme celebrating the thirtieth anniversary in 1987, courtesy of the Patriarch.)

missioner of Police called him in and warned him that his spouse was engaging in behaviour that would ultimately reflect badly on him and his Church. It is unusual that the chief of police in the island was so solicitous of Williams's welfare that he took the time to warn Williams about impending problems with his spouse. But her departure was good fortune for him – or at least he saw it that way. What impact all of this had on the three children is outside the parameters of this story, as they made their futures in Trinidad and not in Barbados. At the same time, however, legitimate curiosity does evoke questions about the impact that this separation from his own family may have had on Williams's ability to offer pastoral support to families in his congregation. There is also little doubt that the absence of a nuclear family surrounding him contributed to persistent and unsubstantiated commentary from outsiders about his being involved with women on the mourning ground. His children have apparently remained members of the Spiritual Baptist faith.

When Williams's wife returned to Trinidad, she reportedly made it clear that she was the Leader of the church in St Ann's. It was also said that she criticized her husband and provoked disagreements in an effort to have him return to Trinidad to resolve them. He detected these ruses, however, and stayed away from that island so as to avoid getting himself into difficulty with her. He has described having a vision in which his wife came to him and asked his forgiveness for having treated him so shabbily. In the vision, he told her that he had long forgiven her, which undoubtedly calmed any concerns he had been experiencing about their failed marriage. The vision may also have helped him justify to himself that the role he played in the dissension within his family was the right one. When his wife died in 1988, he did not attend her funeral.

There are obviously some striking features in this narrative so far that bear remembering and demand extensive consideration. Williams's sense of personal uniqueness properly gave him strength to embark on the enterprise of acting as missionary to his own people in Barbados. No doubt his visions confirmed for him that he was sent by God to deliver the message of salvation. But he was unable to carry out this sacred mission with his wife and children at his side. In interviews on this matter, he seemed quietly contented that he had carried out God's will and that he had played no major part in the ultimate deterioration of his marriage. Whether others, who were witnesses to what transpired in the marriage, would agree with Williams's assessment of things is an important and unanswered question.

CHAPTER 4

The Return to Barbados

AFTER RETURNING TO HIS birthplace in 1957, Granville Williams set about to preach his version of the gospel to the people of Barbados. But his heart must still have been heavy, and not only about the fact that he and his wife obviously did not agree on his decision to be a missionary to Barbados. As the months passed and it was clear that he was not going to return to Trinidad, members of his congregation there sent warnings that he would end up in a Barbados gutter "with dogs licking his face". Perhaps members of the Trinidad congregation, who did not favour his abandoning them, had had their own visions that underscored the importance of his returning to them.

The principal mechanism Williams employed to introduce himself to the Barbados public was the open-air service. Armed with a Bible, bell, lota and the usual gaslight to illuminate his surroundings, Williams conducted church services in areas that were visible to those going about their routine evening activities. At least a modicum of support came from relatives and friends who had known him before he went off to Trinidad. Informants talked enthusiastically about Williams's ability to preach and to explain the Bible, skills that attracted people to him and helped him gradually build up his following. He held open-air services on Monday, Wednesday and Friday evenings, but within a few months a friend offered him a house in the Silver Sands area of Christ Church parish for his first indoor church services. Then, at some time in 1959, Williams moved to the Church in Ealing Grove, which, in the beginning, was much smaller in size than the Cathedral presently located there. Services were then held in church on Sundays and Tuesday and Thursday evenings.

The first years were not easy, by any measure. Williams made his living as a farmer on the extensive land his father had bequeathed him, where he grew vegetables and also established a pig farm. He became progressively better known with every open-air service that he conducted. Certainly he converted some bystanders, just as others simply came out of curiosity to see him and his band of followers. The latter's uniforms of white dresses and head-ties became a trademark, as did their transition into robes of different colours. Several informants recalled their mothers' taking them for entertainment to see this peculiar group that many called "The Tie-Heads". At that time, many people did not see the group as serious about religion. But they liked the rhythmic singing and dancing of the group and wondered what all the bell-ringing was about and why candles were being burnt in the middle of these open-air ceremonies. Bystanders had the definite impression that there wasn't anything predictably religious about the group. Even so, there were mystery and ceremony to their rituals, which only Leader Williams seemed to understand.

Informants noted that the bell ringing and the candles were unusual for Barbadians, as was the rhythmic music that Williams used in his church rituals. Taken together, these observations made many Barbadians think of Obeah or Shango ceremonies, although in reality few Barbadians would have had any direct experience with ceremonies linked to these African belief systems. The connections and associations were made because Williams had brought his novel religious practices from Trinidad. The link between Shango or Orisha ceremonies and Spiritual Baptist ritual will be noted at several points in this narrative in reference to practice in Trinidad. These links have been noted by others over the years (see, for example, Simpson 1980; Ward 1979–1980; Henry 2003; Lum 2000), but it should be clear that Orisha practices have not been accepted even to this day in Barbados.

In my interviews, I also heard on many occasions that Williams was assumed to be the subject of the Mighty Sparrow's popular calypso "Three Coins in the Fountain". (Sparrow is a very well-known calypso singer who was, for many years, a resident in Trinidad.) My informants described the lyrics of this calypso as recounting the story about coins being thrown daily into a fountain by visitors to the site. In the song, the fountain is constructed by a clever Barbadian engineer who knows that Trinidadians are superstitious. As is common in other parts of the world, they throw coins into the water, with the expectation that they will be visited with good luck. Once the money accumulates, however, the "smart Bajan" puts on a bathing suit and dives into the fountain to take out all the coins. The concept of "smart" in this context has been understood as a way of mocking Barbadians, who often unjustifiably suggest that they are cleverer than West Indians from other islands. It therefore seems fair to conclude that Sparrow was at once making fun of Barbadians and possibly also of Williams, who may have created the impression that his success in Trinidad was partly owed to his intellectual superiority over local Leaders.

As the song goes, in the middle of retrieving the coins from the fountain, the thief smugly chortles, "All is mine. All is mine. All is mine." Suspicious Trinidadians eventually understand the trickery, however, and an inspector of police conspires to catch the thief in his very act of deception. The policeman throws three gold coins into the fountain, then goes to hide while waiting to see what the engineer will do. Of course, the Bajan in the story reappears and, as he eyes the gleaming coins, is once again on the verge of gleefully chanting, "All is mine, all is mine." While he wraps his avaricious fingers around the spoils, the police inspector raises his voice with a jeering rasp: "Not this time. Not this time. Not this time." The thief is caught.

It has been a matter of pure speculation for some time whether Sparrow actually intended in his calypso that the "smart Bajan" should be seen as Granville Williams. I say this, as we have few specifics about the Bajan. We only know that he is clever, an engineer, and aware that Trinidadians are superstitious. But there is little doubt that Barbadians have used this idea of the song to suggest that Williams was up to no good in his missionary zeal to convert Barbados. And there is no more effective way to malign a public personality on the island than to ridicule him through the folk medium of a calypso. In fact, some informants argued that the calypso justified their reaching the conclusion that Williams had been forced to leave Trinidad by some unidentified authorities on that island. This vague suggestion that, somewhere on another island, there were charges against Williams that had not yet been formally lodged fuelled speculation about him even more.

As I have previously described, much was made of Williams's alleged sexual involvement with women who joined the new group. But informants also told of their understanding that the women did his bidding and worked as his servants, which led to the belief by non-members of the Church that the women were brainwashed and totally controlled and manipulated by Williams. One woman spoke of a relative who was supposed to be a brilliant student. Once this relative joined the group, she spent an unusual amount of time at the Church and gave up all her usual activities to perform tasks such as sewing Williams's clothes. The informant saw her relative's behaviour as evidence of cult-like tendencies fostered by Williams. Williams's reputation also suffered because of the widespread conviction that it was principally the underclass and the uneducated who were attracted to his message and to membership in this new group. Informants pointed repeatedly to the idea that Williams could lay no claim to having a membership that spread into the middle and upper classes. This has not been a novel finding among scholars of the Spiritual Baptist faith (see, for example, Laitinen 2002 and her observations on Tobago). It is now readily recognized, however, that the socioeconomic status of Williams's followers has improved considerably over the past fifty years (see Griffith, Mahy and Young 2008). Of course, gaining middle- and upper-class followers was an unfair requirement to place on Williams before he was accorded respectability, as many village churches were highly respected even though their members were all poor and struggling. But informants time and again referred to the unusual attire of his members, their use of candles, the ubiquitous bell and the jazzed-up rhythms of their singing as clear evidence of Williams's connection to un-Christian practices. Once his link to Trinidad was revealed, it was sufficient to seal the conclusions.

Despite this state of affairs, Granville Williams kept to his avowed task and returned to Barbados to preach to those who would listen. His youthful energy would not be diluted by sustained, and at times even virulent, criticism from the populace. He knew what people were saying about him, how they were laughing secretly at him. But he held fast to his faith and to his commitment. Williams, like many preachers who are the butt of such criticism, often found solace in the knowledge that Jesus too was persecuted, and he often found strength in the act of praying for those who threw stones at him.

Williams got better at presenting his message with every day's passing. Time also gave him repeated opportunities to explicate his mission, to sharpen his teaching about Spiritual Baptist orthodoxy and to take swipes at the established churches for their failure to attend to the needs of lower-class black people in Barbados. It is true that local churches offered themselves as easy targets. They were rooted in a colonialist teaching that was unapologetic about the position of blacks in comparison to that of whites. Williams had tasted the pleasure of upending this relationship in Trinidad and he could sense that, sooner or later, the idea of a black government would take hold throughout the West Indies. The African countries were beginning to line up for their emancipation, and he believed that the Caribbean's turn was just around the corner.

He dared also to make pronouncements that he sensed would attract some black Bajans to him, just as those same words would alienate others. He knew that he could not and would not be ignored forever – especially not when he said that Jesus was black, as were many of the other mainline prophets. The veracity of his assertions weren't even important after a while, because he learned to couch his claims in the theory that the established churches had hidden the simple, straightforward truth from black people for a long time. Pointing to the glory of bygone black civilizations, he urged blacks to read about their historical origins. Through the unique rituals of the Spiritual Baptist faith, he demonstrated that blacks could develop a direct connection to God and the angels. He showed how God would speak directly to black people through their visions and dreams and explained that white intermediaries were not necessary for blacks to enter the kingdom of heaven. As he made his arguments, he showed that there were many mysteries kept hidden from those who would not undertake to live a truly spiritual life. The message presented in this way by Williams reflects to some extent the invention and creativity mentioned by Chatfield (1998) and Laitinen (2002) in their characterization of Spiritual Baptist efforts to present a new or differently packaged message to their members.

The first step in attaining the spiritual life that Williams spoke of was to be baptized through immersion. I have already mentioned the story of Philip and the eunuch as a mere symbol of the significance of this first step. According to Spiritual Baptist belief, as one's faith and commitment deepens, it is logical to take the path to mourning. It is in this ritual that a convert senses the very proximity of God through manifestations of the Holy Spirit in the form of visions in which conversations can be held with the Master, the angels and the saints of old. Granville Williams's enunciations could not be ignored, as can be seen in one informant's account that, when he was contemplating being baptized by Leader Williams, the local Anglican bishop made it clear that being baptized by Williams would mean that the informant was no longer an Anglican. Such stories suggest strongly that Williams was making progress and that even the powerful Anglican Church was fearful of his inroads into their family of believers.

Still, the road was rocky. Some new converts to Williams's movement were ostracized by their own families. One individual I interviewed explained that, while he was still an adolescent in high school, his parents excluded him from the home after they learned that he had joined Williams's group. Members were cautious about wearing their head-ties in public. Cruel bystanders sometimes tugged at these scarves and made fun of those wearing them. It was even reported that some families threw water on the robes worn by their relatives who had joined the new movement. This kind of persecution was also reported to have extended to the workplace, where members of the movement were shunned and made to understand that their conversion to this new religion was a sign of silliness. Williams himself was not exempt from these acts of disrespectful condemnation. Some were more overt than others.

For example: Williams has related how, in those early years, he had performed a burial ceremony in the churchyard of an Anglican church, and bystanders were looking to see how he would handle the necessary signing of the government documents that were required at the completion of the service. His critics expected him to "get lock up" by the police for having illegally conducted the burial. But Williams knew from his years in Trinidad that it was important to register with the authorities so that he could perform weddings and funerals. Since he was acutely aware of the regulations and was confident that he had obtained the requisite authority, he went about his business confidently. He expected to surprise his detractors when he calmly signed the documents. But it hurt him to know that his own people had not yet developed trust in him as a man of God.

As time went by, Williams's theological teachings began to seem more concordant with the race-based changes that had swept Europe and the Americas and were now reaching the Caribbean. Barbados gained independence in 1966 and, a few years later, talk was in full swing about black power. Suddenly, all that Williams was preaching took on added relevance. Everyday discourse became more focused on what was indigenous to Barbados and the Caribbean. As the tide of public opinion and awareness gradually turned, the Spiritual Baptist movement had more claims to legitimacy in Barbados than did the Anglican Church. Even theologically, Williams appeared more thoughtful and creatively useful to the emerging black populace that had suddenly found a voice in Barbadian culture. At least he was talking pointedly about the redemption of black people and saying that they had a legitimate place in heaven near to their black Redeemer. And the black populace took up the refrain against Eurocentrism and idolatrous claims that Jesus and Abraham and many others were white. I will leave to others the task of demonstrating whether Williams's claims in this regard are demonstrably true or false. What is of import here is that his assertions found attentive ears in the climate of post-independence Barbados.

I have found it instructive throughout the years to think of Williams as a teacher. As I have come to understand his didactic approach, he assumed that the traditional churches did not do a good job of explicating the mysteries available to the Afro-Caribbean population in the context of the Christian religion. Hence, he thought it necessary to clarify for the non-initiated what, for example, the Bible had to offer. But then he took additional pleasure and pride in holding up the Spiritual Baptist faith as a faith with secrets. One could, however, learn these secrets with the passage of time and with devotion to studying the tenets of the faith; no one could learn it all in a few weeks or months. Furthermore, Williams cautioned any hasty and curious Church members to proceed with spiritual respect in setting about to deepen their knowledge of Spiritual Baptist rituals and beliefs. I heard him explain in a sermon that inexperienced members should not participate in certain ceremonies within the Church. He insisted that the uninitiated should "keep out of higher heights", and went on to note, "A child cannot do a man's work." He excoriated those who would "step in front when they don't know what they are doing". As an example, he cited the simple task of taking up a shepherd's rod, a common wooden staff used by Spiritual Baptists in their rituals. He explained that one must know the appropriate way to pick up the rod and to put it down before proceeding to touch the implement.

In my interviews of other clergy who were not members of the Spiritual Baptist faith, several agreed that Williams's teachings about the relationship between blacks and Christianity drew Barbadians to him. Indeed, they noted that Williams had stepped into a void that had been scrupulously avoided by the older established denominations, and they saw him as a reminder of the roles being played by independent churches in Africa: he was confronting the dogma espoused by white-dominated faith groups; he offered an alternative linked to a newly aggressive respect for things black; and he celebrated this voyage of self-discovery that would help members to renounce colonial subservience and discover a new pride in the Afro-Barbadian. My clergy sources also noted that Williams's unusual message added, over time, a distinctive patina to his already marked charismatic nature.

As I have come to appreciate after years of following Williams, he dispenses knowledge about Spiritual Baptist philosophy in carefully titrated doses that are, at most times, controlled by him. It is important that his followers acknowledge his superior knowledge and the fact that they have learned from him. Of course, I have seen this mandate in many other religious groups and in non-religious organizations as well. But in the hierarchical structure of the Spiritual Baptist faith, the deepening of one's belief and knowledge is not entirely under one's individual control. It is essential to maintain humility in the displays of one's experience, particularly in front of one's own spiritual father.

Not surprisingly, Williams has been criticized for not being willing to give up control, even after he has ostensibly appointed someone to a particular role within his organization. In the words of one person I interviewed, Williams's attitude may lead at times to the spiritual stagnation of those willing to take on responsibility within the group. As that individual saw it, Williams will appoint you to a particular post, but then will require you to sit quietly until he instructs you how to carry out even the simplest of your duties. He will do this even though he knows full well that you have the knowledge and experience to carry out your assignments and fulfil his instructions competently. This same point of criticism was repeated by several other Church members I interviewed.

Williams has been quite aware of this kind of criticism, and he concedes that such commentary has been painful to him in the past. It seems clear that he has, over the years, confronted criticism from sources external to the Church more effectively than he has dealt with censure emanating from Church members, perhaps because external critique can always be categorized as similar to what Jesus endured from those who resisted His teachings. In other words, external commentary is expected and must be endured as the price of eventual success. Internal rebukes are seen more as a form of treachery, while, at the same time, they more eloquently characterize one's failure to maintain a cadre of disciples committed to one's teachings. No doubt, it is also easier to label external rebukes as uninformed and unjustified than to say the same thing glibly about those who, in an earlier time, were shouting one's praises.

In a wonderful vignette that conflates the theme of external criticism and his power to overcome it, Williams told me the story of a man who had threatened to shoot him because of his problematic Spiritual Baptist teachings. One day, the man fell ill with a stroke. The family accused Williams of having performed Obeah to make the man sick. At a later point, in a gesture of magnanimity, Williams went to pray for the man, and the individual's condition got better. At this sign of improvement, the still-angry family maintained that Williams's success was quite understandable. They grasped the obvious, in referring to Williams: "He know how to get he better because he put he so."

The internal criticism is now more astutely organized and better informed, although uncovering it was not an easy task. It is focused on Williams's clear centralization of power and authority and his capacity to camouflage the vertical dimension of what at first appears to be a horizontal democratization of his leadership style. For example, in the Spiritual Baptist rituals generally, church members participate in reading lessons, leading prayers, picking up the lota and ringing the bells at will, as the Spirit moves them. Behind that apparent global participation, however, is often a tightly run organization. In the case of Williams, some have suggested that he wields his authority with a practised opaqueness that is often only pierced by the experienced analytic eye. It is also said that young members question why they should literally bow when they encounter Williams. And even I was surprised once when I saw a distinguished professional stand to address Williams in a casual conversation. I have never once seen anyone interrupt Williams when he was speaking.

This matter of his closely held power raises prickly questions that are commonly expected in the examination of authority dynamics exercised in organizations. Some observers noted that Williams's tendency to hold many cards close to the vest is manifest in different ways. At one funeral service I observed, it seemed quite clear that everyone was ready to proceed with the ritual, including the bereaved family and the undertaker. Since Williams had not yet appeared, however, his assisting clergy kept everyone waiting. Finally, one of the clergy went and told him that by his absence he was holding up the proceedings. Williams apparently replied that they should have started and he would join them. Bystanders who were members of the Church, however, told me that the Leader knew very well that no one would start a service with outsiders present if he had not explicitly given his consent for things to proceed – an example of authority being closely held concerning minor matters. Williams has been known to make clear his ideas about more important subjects, however.

For example, members of the Church have run afoul of Williams's principle that those clergy who represent him in the performance of certain rituals must do so with a persistent humility. They must always be concerned about whether they are overstepping the boundary that must contain their enthusiasm and unconscious wish to shine as competent clergy. In certain cases, the clergy have begun to develop a reputation for distinctive competence and have then found themselves being put "on the backbench" to learn more about humility and simplicity. To be on the backbench, of course, is to be publicly humiliated and to be forced to give up temporarily the privilege of participating in ecclesiastical rituals. It is not a punishment easily digested by proud men and women who have already risen to visible heights in the organization.

It should be noted at this point that the backbench phenomenon is not limited to Williams and his faith group. Several Barbadian members of other churches have explained that, in their denominations, individuals were put on the backbench for a number of reasons, such as adultery, getting pregnant while unmarried and so on. It is clear that a number of denominations in Barbados utilize the backbench mechanism as a way of maintaining discipline, punishing infractions and reinforcing the point that there exists a vertical hierarchy in the organization.

The comments about Williams's tendency to be authoritarian are not easily dissected. His supporters are more numerous than his detractors, at least within the Church. So it is not surprising that I found his most vocal critics outside the membership, although there are a few members who are not totally enamoured of his management style. The outside critics point to his way of conducting general meetings attended by Church members, especially that part of the meeting that might reasonably be called a trial. In trials, a complainant usually states that a member of the Church has transgressed some established principle. It is then expected that the respondent will defend himself. Ultimately, Williams as Leader makes a determination of the respondent's guilt or innocence and issues a punishment that is usually linked to some form of taking the backbench.

Some have said that, as simultaneous judge and jury, Williams can at times be capricious and lack objectivity. He may also be as emotional as the average person and be swayed by witnesses whom he likes. From time to time, he has been seen as unusually arbitrary and unbending, as in a case where he "dismissed" a member from Church duties without specifying whether that punishment was temporary or permanent. It was also reported that he did not and would not inform the member from which particular activities the member was to be excluded. In another case, a member was put on the back bench for fifty years, which seemed an inordinately long punishment to many of those present at the hearing.

Williams has remained content that he meted out these punishments with the guidance of the Holy Spirit. In his view, they were proportionate to the severity of the transgressions. In response to questions from a member about the justification for such punishments, Williams is said to have replied that he would not die like the Old Testament's Eli, a Hebrew priest in 1 Samuel 4 who failed to correct his sons' sinful behaviour. After being told that his sons had been murdered and the Ark of the Covenant captured, Eli fell backwards and died of a broken neck. The Church member who questioned Williams's severity saw Williams's use of this metaphorical reference to Eli's death as a leader's justification for applying sanctions, even those that may be seen as unduly onerous and painful. Williams was thought to be arguing that a leader is not allowed to shrink from these unpleasant duties, as it is required that he be responsible for the spiritual welfare of his flock. In taking these responsibilities seriously, he must mete out punishment as God would have him do through the motivation of the Holy Spirit.

Even Williams's detractors, however, concede that he is possessed of remarkable charisma and presence when he is conducting a Spiritual Baptist ritual. He moves with serenity and ease. He controls everything within hearing of his voice. He directs his trusted aides with a barely perceptible flick of the wrist and he instinctively knows the hymn that will calm his audience and the one that will have people going into the spirit. He also has the distinctive ability to "raise a hymn" at judicious junctures in the service. The Spiritual Baptist tradition of raising a hymn requires one to start singing the first verse of the hymn from memory. The congregation then joins the singing, and an assistant may use a hymn book to read each line just before it is sung. The one who raises the hymn must, however, sing the two lines or so with confidence, exhibiting knowledge of the words as well as the tune. In some services,

Williams may raise more than ten hymns himself, which requires a prodigious memory and unbridled confidence.

Comment will also be made later about Williams's exercise of his discretionary authority in blessing garments to be worn by specific members (see chapter 7). No member may wear a Church vestment that has not been specifically authorized by Williams himself. I was impressed that my informants in the clergy who were not members of Williams's congregation were consistently complimentary in describing his ability to handle himself in the midst of his church ritual. They saw him as unusually charismatic and were in awe of his technical use of theatre and drama in his direction of church rituals.

I have already made reference to visions and dreams described by Granville Williams and have noted that I will explain later the fundamental importance of dreams and visions in the Spiritual Baptist faith. Still, it is useful here to reemphasize that dreams and visions also played a role in the unfolding of Williams's life. As he struggled to impose his new faith group on the broader Barbadian society, it would be expected that he would welcome support from any quarter. And for Spiritual Baptists, guidance from the Holy Spirit would be especially sought and appreciated, particularly through the medium of dreams and visions.

Williams has reported that, in this context of expectation, he experienced a dream in which he was talking to Jesus, who said, "Men will fight against you. But they cannot win. I am with you." Jesus continued, "I will never leave you in this world or the next." This reaffirmation of a particular commitment to Williams as pastor and to his work as a missionary was catalyst enough to sustain him in his times of doubt and fatigue. These themes would return as Williams obviously sought confirmation that he was on the right track and recognition that he was a chosen man of God.

Williams explained that, in another vision, he was walking to church when he looked back and saw a big dragon coming to devour him. The dragon was about to strike when Williams felt the touch of a hand on his right shoulder. He looked and saw the Master smiling and saying, "Do not be afraid of him. He cannot harm you." With the Master's hand on his shoulder, Williams continued walking. He saw this vision later on as a wonderfully reinvigorating experience. No doubt, he could feel it as a unique protective web against the slings and arrows of his detractors.

Williams's self-doubt and its calming were visible in yet another vision, in which he grabbed the feet of Jesus and begged, "Lord, bless me." Jesus replied, "You are already blessed. Go and do my Father's work." Williams was content to derive strength as much from this intimate contact with Jesus as from the words that confirmed his standing in the spiritual world. Others may, quite naturally, trivialize these spiritual interactions as childish manifestations of wish fulfilment. But after years of discussing dreams and visions with Spiritual Baptists, I have found no way to pierce the veil of their beliefs in this regard.

It is clear that, with the passage of time, things got better for Granville Williams. The progress of his missionary efforts was enhanced and the Church became more widely known and progressively more popular. Williams was consecrated bishop in 1978 by then-Archbishop Griffith of Trinidad, who later raised Williams himself to the ecclesiastical rank of archbishop on 24 January 1988. Griffith and his colleagues (2008) have noted that, in addition to Williams's personal achievements, there is now strong consensus about his Church's current positive standing in the broader Barbadian community. Such progress in fact contradicts the expectation of other observers (see, for example, Chatfield 1998) about the eventual success of the Spiritual Baptist movement in the Caribbean.

Evidence of this progress can be seen in the faith group's improved financial resources, as witnessed by their successful building programme and their impressive numbers at public events; their enhanced visibility, seen through their participation in national cultural programmes; their being viewed as an institution that represents black people's secular and spiritual interests; their raising of their members' socioeconomic status; and their visible connection to the island's political leadership. These points buttress Williams's pride that the organization he has built is now much better integrated into Barbadian society and is recognized as a distinctive and distinguished part of the local culture. (Or, to put it in the terms of Professor Frances Henry [2003], Williams's Church has undergone the process of socio-political legitimation in the context of Barbadian society.) He has clearly worked to render these accomplishments permanent. For example, informants have pointed out that he has taken steps to make the Church more friendly and accessible. He welcomes the use of cameras in his services and is open to inquiries from the media. He has even opened up, on occasion, the secret mourning ground to visits from outsiders. With these subtle changes, the Church is clearly becoming less of a secret organization and more of an organization with a few secrets.

Williams's connection to political leaders has been the subject of some discussion between him and me. I have often wondered whether he was tempted to seek political office. My curiosity arose for obvious reasons: Williams was familiar with the potential for the use of a healthy Spiritual Baptist congregation as a grass-roots organization that could influence political parties and candidates; he had values and interests that could be employed to influence the platform of a given political party; he was interested in taking a hand in the development of post-independence black Caribbean governments; and he understood firsthand that politicians and clergy could be comfortable bedfellows in a Caribbean that so readily melded the secular and the religious. Still, Williams insisted to me that once he left Trinidad, and despite the entreaties and invitations from a number of Barbadian politicians, he swore off politics. Or rather, he decided to give up any individual participation in the political platforms of Barbados.

It is obvious from even brief and superficial conversations with Williams that he knows the influence that the leader of a vibrant and large congregation can have on those who have political clout in any Caribbean island. Furthermore, he knows that certain privileges in Barbadian society can only be obtained through appeals to those in political power. He does not flaunt the connections he may have to politicians. But many of my informants have certainly drawn the conclusion that he could not participate in the many nationally visible activities that witness his attendance if he were in the political wilderness. He has connections, they say. And the Archbishop will add no more information to make things clearer. I draw the conclusion that he exercises his influence with discretion and with subtlety. After all, there is no distinct advantage to his letting everyone know what strings he may be able to pull when it is necessary to do so. In addition, his diplomacy and discretion allow him to be the friend of all, instead of being painted as the partisan follower of a political party.

CHAPTER 5

On Faith and Ritual

WHENEVER I ENTER A Spiritual Baptist service these days, I am struck by a sense of awe, particularly now that we are in the twenty-first century. I often wonder about the closing days of the nineteenth-century Caribbean, and as I try to focus on what must have been the nature of rituals then, with the powerful presence of Africa, the intimidating presence of whatever microcosmic religious influence was permitted by former slave masters to permeate services conducted by blacks, my imagination does not capture much. I have fractured images from pictures of Spiritual Baptists attending pilgrimages in Trinidad, for example, some time in the early or late 1940s, with men attired in simple robes and women dressed in short white dresses and head-ties. They were fighting against difficult odds, practicing a religion that ran afoul of the authorities until 1951, and in facilities that must be unimaginable to most Barbadians in 2009. I admire those who preceded us, given all that they were struggling against, including the poverty and the colonial status of second-class citizens in a developing country.

My surprise at the changes I have witnessed in the Barbados Spiritual Baptist Church over the years has grown, especially as I have begun to appreciate more comprehensively what adherents of the faith have achieved in recent decades. I credit my increasing surprise to my gradual maturation in comprehension of the rituals, symbols and beliefs of the faith. Still, it is worthwhile to keep in mind an important characteristic of the Spiritual Baptist faith – that the leader of every Spiritual Baptist church experiments and creates a new flourish here and a different flourish there in the ritual of the faith group under his charge. In this chapter, I would like to explain the basic faith tenets and rituals of the Barbadian Spiritual Baptists through experiential accounts of Church members and descriptions of services that I have attended.

ROUTES TO MEMBERSHIP

Individuals over the years have utilized different routes in establishing contact with the Barbados Church and then eventually joining it. Given the Church's age at present, a number of families have had trans-generational membership. Consequently, adult members of these families have described themselves as having been born into the Church. By that is meant that, as youngsters, they were taken to services by their mothers who were Church members. Then, usually as adolescents, they were baptized after formally declaring their decision to join the faith.

In addition to this group whose Church membership was partly handed down to them from an older generation, there are others who came to membership in an uncomplicated fashion. For example, a well-educated adolescent male explained that he used to attend a Pentecostal church as an obligation to his mother. When it came time for him to make his own decision about a church, he chose the Spiritual Baptists. He reached his decision after attending a Church pageant at the invitation of a friend. He enjoyed the liveliness of the group and felt very satisfied, so he opted for the Spiritual Baptists. He made his decision without being under any duress and without the stimulus of a vision.

There is another way to membership that usually relies on the catalytic effect of a vision or dream. For example, an individual explained to me the decision to join the Church in its very early days. This member had a dream about going to the Church and encountering the pastor, who was waiting there to pray for this individual. The person ignored this first dream and did nothing about it. The dream came again, however, and this time the individual decided to obey and join the movement. This example highlights the role played by dreams in the Spiritual Baptist faith.

Not all future Church members have taken, under the influence of a dream or vision, such a direct route to joining the Church. Ms A (not the initial of her real name) talked of sensing a general malaise about her life and progressively realizing that she was a sinner and needed to change things. She described feeling increasing pressure to make a decision. So, after inadvertently letting a broom fall one day while she was engaged in sweeping, she saw it as an inescapable sign that the time had come. She dropped to her knees and prayed. She made the decision to give her life to Christ and asked God to indicate a choice of church that she should attend.

Afterwards, Ms A had a dream in which she saw herself attending the Spiritual Baptist Church. She identified the particular religious denomination by the garments worn by members of the congregation. She realized that the dream was indicating God's choice for her and she started to attend the Church. She still remained hesitant about joining the group until she had another dream in which the Leader came to her and expressed his disappointment about her continuing hesitancy. She felt ashamed and scolded. The dream gave her strength to persevere and not long after, at an evening service, she went to the mercy seat. This action was a declared, public acknowledgement of her decision to join the faith, as the mercy seat is a bench on which potential members sit with arms outstretched and palms turned upwards in a position of supplication and repentance. The position at once signifies an openness to God and to receiving the Holy Spirit, while also translating a certain personal humility and a request for the remission of sins. She took the next important step toward full membership by being baptized a few weeks later.

Mr B (not the initial of his real name) was attending a funeral when he had a vision that came to him while Spiritual Baptist members attending the interment were chanting in their usual way. In the vision he was suddenly lifted into the air and started flying around. He enjoyed the experience and stated that it "was the most beautiful experience I ever had". He could not explain why the feeling had come over him and he reported that it lasted about fifteen minutes. He had never attended a Spiritual Baptist funeral before. The vision influenced him to conclude later that the Spiritual Baptist Church was the one he should attend. About a week after his vision, he went to the Church, and during the service a Mother of the Church invited him to the altar, where they prayed together. This act cemented his decision to join the faith, and he was later baptized.

The decision to join the Church may therefore be relatively straightforward and may arise as a matter of course because the individual has grown up attending services in the Church with close relatives. This type of membership could be considered a primary membership, since there often appears to be no obvious catalytic event driving the decision. In the case of secondary membership, the decision is facilitated by some personal experience of the individual, which in many cases is related to a dream or vision that the individual has had. The vision is especially likely to occur when the person is actually seeking help in choosing a church. Faced with this problem, it appears that some Barbadians are accustomed to waiting for God to declare His wish through this medium of the Holy Spirit. At first, I was under the impression that waiting for answers through visions was the hallmark of Spiritual Baptists. But my interviews have demonstrated quite clearly that many Spiritual Baptist members actually have their first encounters with visions before becoming members of the Church. An experience with visions that predates joining the Church may in fact be advantageous to future members, as they will certainly find out, in the process of becoming a Church member, that the Spiritual Baptist faith holds dreams and visions in high regard, and these latter experiences occupy an important place in the beliefs and customs of the Church. The important point here, of course, is that the Barbadian culture itself supports the idea of using dreams and visions in one's daily life, so that the Spiritual Baptist faith seems to reinforce their roles rather than to create them anew.

BAPTISM

Once one has expressed a willingness to join the Church, the individual attends services and sits on the mercy seat as a probationary member of the group, as I have described above. Full membership, however, is gained through the ritual of baptism, which must be done in a body of living water because, as it was explained to me, life begets life. Consequently, stagnant water should not be used for a baptismal service. Baptism is not to be confused with the christening of children, which usually takes place in many different denominations a few weeks after the birth of the child. Christening is the occasion when parents and godparents commit themselves to raising the child in a Christian manner. It may also be the formal point at which the child is named. But for the Spiritual Baptists, to christen a child is not to baptize him. They think of baptism in terms of what John the Baptist did to Jesus, as described

Figure 5.1 Archbishop Williams holding a child to be christened. Font is at left. Barbados, 2008.

at Matthew 2:16–17, or Philip's baptism of the Ethiopian eunuch at Acts 8:36–39. In the case of the eunuch, he confessed his belief that Jesus Christ is the Son of God (v. 37), which Spiritual Baptists hold as a fundamental expression of what is necessary for baptism.

I recall engaging in a conversation with several young men at the site of a Barbados Spiritual Baptist baptism. They explained, with the vehement bravado typical of Barbadian men when they are engaged in an earnest argument that they can feel they won't win easily, that the only way to a true Christian life is through baptism. As one said, with the enthusiastic support of the others, "Baptism is the only way." They buttressed this assertion by pointing out that even God attended the baptism of Jesus and displayed His presence when He said, "This is my beloved son in whom I am well pleased."

The time between initially joining the Church and being baptized may vary from one individual to another. Spiritual Baptists like to say that the time of baptism is dictated by the moving of the Holy Spirit, but other factors obviously intervene. For example, in some churches, the person leading the group may not have received the spiritual gift permitting him to baptize others (this gift, like many others, is conferred by the Holy Spirit during a dream or vision), and the leader is therefore required to ask a baptizer from another church to help. The Archbishop in Barbados claims the gift; however, he tends to baptize his candidates at specific times, such as on Palm Sunday. So individuals joining the Church may have to wait for the propitious moment at which the Leader prefers to baptize. At first I assumed that only adults having the obvious competence to express the belief in Jesus Christ would be baptized. But I interviewed several Church members who were baptized as children when they had not even reached the age of six years. They had been in the Church as babes in arms, and their stating that they wanted to be baptized was accepted by the Leader as a special manifestation of the Holy Spirit.

In a baptismal service I attended in 2008, the baptismal candidates were all sitting on the mercy seat (the length of a typical school bench) during the service. Testimonies were given by older members of the Church about the significance of baptism. One member explained that baptism was a form of death that was followed by an ultimate rebirth. Another pointed out that baptism marks the entrance to the Spiritual Baptist faith and that it is also a precondition for mourning, a ceremony discussed later in this chapter. Other

Figure 5.2 Female candidates for baptism dressed in simple blue robes. Nurses are in blue and white attire. Barbados, 2008.

members testified that baptism had dramatically changed their lives and put them on the pathway of living for Christ.

Eventually, the Leader appeared and took charge of this part of the service. He blessed basins of water and added oil to them. Then he passed in front of the candidates and ceremoniously washed each candidate's hands. An Abbess of the Church followed and washed the feet of each candidate. The Archbishop then returned and anointed each candidate with oil: head and face, then hands. At this point, the Abbess returned. She took a white band off the shoulder of an assistant and placed the band on the right shoulder of each candidate. The Leader then passed back and anointed each candidate's feet with oil. He returned to take the white band off each candidate's shoulder and tie it around each candidate's head.

From behind, an assistant pressed a long, white rod against both of each candidate's shoulders. Other assistants placed, in turn, a cross and a shepherd's crook (a staff with a hook at one end) on the candidates' shoulders. The Abbess then passed back and pressed a lota, a Bible and a bell on each candidate: on

Figure 5.3 Congregation at beach for baptismal ceremony. Visible in the altar are crosses, shepherd's crook and simple rod; bell is on the sand. Barbados, 2008.

Figure 5.4 Altar at baptismal ceremony. Visible on sand are bells, lotas and candle. Barbados, 2008.

the heart, head, shoulders, back and abdomen. The touching of these anatomical areas readily evokes Paul's recommendation in his Letter to the Ephesians that they take on "the whole armour of God" (Ephesians. 6:11). The elements used in this part of the ceremony, such as the lota and bell, are known to be the tools of the Spiritual Baptists. While this ceremonial activity was taking place, members of the Church were singing different hymns and chants. It was also quite striking how much organized movement, involving a significant number of Church members, was occurring simultaneously. At that point in the service, I counted the presence of about 350 people. Eventually, the mood became distinctively calm. A text was read from the Bible, another quiet hymn was sung and all the members prepared for the procession to the beach where the actual baptism would take place. In this case they went to Miami Beach, located in the parish of Christ Church; however, other venues on the island have been used in the past for baptisms.

At the beach, the candidates for baptism were lined up fairly close to the aligned tools of the Church, such as the lota, bell, crosses, shepherd's crook and Church flag. The alignment of the tools on the sand looked like a make-

Figure 5.5 Young baptismal candidate being led from sea after immersion, preceded by cross-bearer. Barbados, 2008.

shift altar. Each candidate walked into the sea, accompanied by a supporter, towards the Archbishop, who first blessed the water with a rod and cross, and the blessing was accompanied by the ringing of a hand bell. He then baptized each candidate, who was afterwards escorted out of the sea by a supporter.

It was a glorious event, irresistible to tourists who just happened to be there observing, and equally touching to local Barbadians who had known the event was going to take place and had come to watch things unfold. It was hard to remain unmoved by the orderliness, the pageantry, the disciplined hymn-singing, and the multi-coloured robes worn by the members on the beach. In addition, the sun at the time was gently receding behind the horizon in the far distance, and the crepuscular light danced magically off the waves. It was the kind of evening that evoked gasps of awe from the witnesses there. I felt I could read their thoughts that said, "Only God could create such beauty." One male bystander on the beach walked up to a Church member and, almost weeping, asked to be baptized by the Leader. His wish was granted. Another member filled a bell with seawater and gave it to her children to drink. She wanted the benefits of blessed water for her offspring. Similarly, another member asked one of the ministers to wash her feet in the blessed seawater. She told me it was for the pain in her feet. The ceremonial procession left the beach around seven o'clock that evening, and the members slowly wended their way back to the Church. They reached the Church almost two hours later.

When they arrived at the Church, the front door was closed. Someone read a scripture passage. The Archbishop knocked three times. Someone inside the Church asked, "Who goes there?" I could not hear the Archbishop's response, but the door was opened. Several readings then took place. The first began with the well-known "I will lift up mine eyes unto the hills". Another was "I was glad when they said unto me let us go into the house of the Lord". The Archbishop finally did his reading in plainsong, which reminded me of Gregorian chanting I had heard in Catholic services. After that, the baptismal candidates entered the Church under an arch formed by a cross and a shepherd's crook. They went in procession around the Church several times, as the Leader stayed in the centre of the Church and directed the singing of hymns. Finally the candidates returned to the mercy seat at the front of the Church. The Leader addressed the candidates and told them that through baptism they had become saints in the Church. He encouraged them to let their spiritual light shine before men and stated that, from then on, they were transformed in the Spirit.

The Archbishop then blessed each candidate anew with oil, which he put on the head, forehead and hands. He also wrote a seal on their palms in the ritual practice of sealing, in which the Archbishop writes or draws a pattern of some sort on the material or person to be "sealed". The seal itself is a spiritual symbol that is meant to protect or bless. Examples of seals are a cross, rod and ladder. Some seals are familiar to most members. Others are held in thorough secrecy by those using them and are rarely explained to members below a certain Church rank. After being sealed, each candidate was banded afresh with a white band; females had a head-tie placed on top of the band. The Leader then passed back and gave each candidate a password, which is always held secret by the person who receives it. Like seals, passwords are derived from biblical practices and are used by each member to fend off spiritual difficulties and problems. When Jesus, in the midst of his trials in the wilderness, told the devil, "Get thee behind me, Satan", he is said to have used that expression as a password. Following this part of the ritual, the candidates were invited to give testimonies about their experiences during baptism.

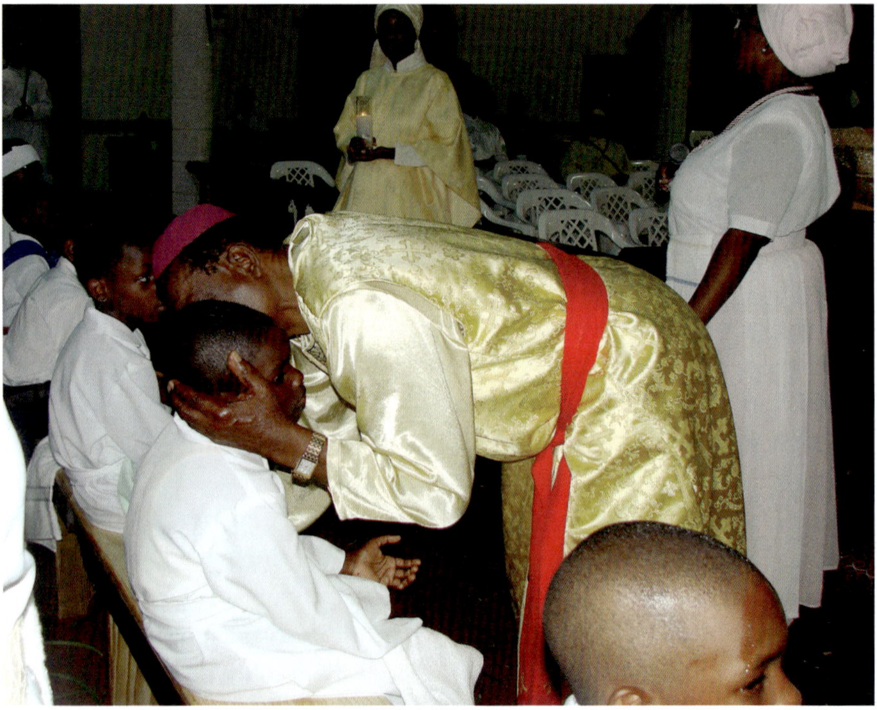

Figure 5.6 Leader giving the secret password to a baptismal candidate. Barbados, 2008.

The password is also referred to by some members as a "key". The technical facility with which one can use a password is a sign of one's depth of spirituality. In explanation of this point, a member described a dream that he had, in which he was on his way to Jerusalem when Satan appeared in front of him and barred his way. At first the member was worried, but then he realized that he was in possession of his key. He uttered the password, but he emphasized that he did it "with his whole being", a mechanism that substantially increased its power and effectiveness. He was taken aback to see that Satan immediately began to recede in size. And as that happened, Satan gave him a look of recognition that showed that he had known that the member belonged to a Spiritual Baptist group possessing power in the spirit world. I have long given up trying to explain to outsiders how Spiritual Baptists think about these things. Suffice it to say that the password is part of their belief system, and it occupies a prominent place. In addition, members utilize their passwords with more or less confidence, depending on their experience and accumulated success over time. They also point out that the password is helpful in negotiating difficult situations in their day-to-day secular lives.

After dispensing passwords, the Archbishop moved to the ritual of proving, which is part of the baptismal ceremony. In this ritual, a Bible is placed in the hands of each candidate. The candidates open the Bibles in turn, with their right and left thumbs falling on specific verses somewhere within it. These verses are then read. Following the reading of each candidate's verses, the Archbishop begins to sing a hymn that is said to be transmitted to him by the Holy Spirit and is meant to be the hymn designated specifically for that particular candidate. This hymn is expected to be used by the new member in moments of temptation or weakness. The hymn provides the candidate with strength, as does the password that the Leader has already whispered in that candidate's ear. Examples of hymns given that night were: "Lead kindly light amid the encircling gloom, lead thou me on"; "God moves in a mysterious way His wonders to perform"; "There shall be showers of blessing, this is the promise of love"; "Rock of ages cleft for me". Each hymn was sung softly and in a way that clearly suggested it was meant to provide balm for the suffering.

Figure 5.7 Baptismal candidate undergoing proving. Barbados, 2008.

Proving is used to determine the approximate spiritual level of a given person or even that person's spiritual future in the Church. Spiritual Baptists have pointed out to me that Jesus himself was proved at Luke 4:16–20, which describes Jesus as entering the synagogue and standing up to read, when someone gives Him the book of the prophet Esaias. He opens the book and finds the place where it is written, "The spirit of the Lord is upon me." The central point here is that Jesus is believed to have opened the book to precisely the spot that captured His profound spirituality and that demonstrated who He was in a spiritual sense. Proving in the Spiritual Baptist orthodoxy is also seen in the mourning ritual.

Following the ritual of proving in the baptismal ceremony, members took the candidates to each of the four corners of the Church, which also represent the four corners of the world. First was the corner where a red flag was hung to signify victory and represent the Archangel Michael; then the yellow corner of power and the Archangel Gabriel; next was the green corner of life and the Archangel Uriel; and finally the blue corner of glory and the Archangel Raphael. Flags are a common symbol in Spiritual Baptist churches, although they occupy a more prominent place in some churches than in others.

The candidates were then invited to give testimonial impressions of their experiences during the baptismal ceremony. Some candidates talked of what God had done for them in their lives. One discussed coming to God after a bout with cancer. Another had taken the step to baptism after being depressed. One person described turning and twisting in a lost way before finding the true way to Christ. Another candidate explained being invited to the Church by a member. The candidate had attended a service and was surprised by the warmth of the welcome; no one seemed concerned with how the candidate was dressed, and that person acknowledged the warm feeling experienced during the service. None of the testimonials on that day described any unusual visions.

After testimonies were given, another hymn was sung and the Church was surveyed once again during that service. In Spiritual Baptist belief, the ritual surveying of a church sanctuary may be used to drive away evil spirits and sanctify the building. At other times, as on this occasion, surveying is carried out as an act of celebrating and glorifying God. Usually, a member carrying a lota in the left hand and a bell in the right proceeds to the corners of the building. At each corner, water from the lota is poured onto the floor and the bell is also rung. This process is repeated at the other corners and the foot of the Church, which is the main entrance to the building. It is also done at the centre-pole area of the sanctuary. We shall return later to the lota and the bell, two fundamental tools of the Spiritual Baptists (see "Symbols and Tools" in chapter 6).

Once the church had been surveyed, the adult male candidates were directed to sit with the group of members called the Knights, and the adult females were taken to sit with the League of Mary. The male children sat with the Sacred Hearts, and the female children joined the Rosebuds (see table 1 in chapter 8). The baptismal ceremony had then run its course, and the service gradually drew to a close.

A FRIDAY NIGHT SERVICE

I have tried to imagine the reaction of a new member to all the pageantry and ritual observed in the Spiritual Baptist Church, and I suspect that some people are entranced by it just as others are numbed by its complexity. The services are subdivided into mini-rituals that are carried out by a number of different members. The participation of a broad cross-section of the congregation in the Church services may well be a point of attraction for those who are new to the Church. Each mini-ritual has a meaning that is often impenetrable to the outsider, a fact that adds to the mysterious halo that surrounds the Spiritual Baptist faith. In each ritual, tools and symbols are used that again carry meaning not known to everybody. Mystery and knowledge increase with experience and being spiritually attuned to the moving of the Holy Spirit. I will now review here how some of the Church rituals unfold in the context of a common Friday night service.

This service, as I observed it, took place at the smaller Church in Richmond Gap, St Michael, between seven and ten o'clock in the evening. It was directed by several of the male ministers. A Bishop was present, as were several Abbesses. The Archbishop was not there. As the time drew near for the service to begin, three males went to kneel down and pray in the centre aisle of the Church. One carried a shepherd's crook. The other two had wooden swords in their hands. After praying, one man went to a side entrance to guard the Church with his sword. The other two, with sword and staff, went to stand at the main entrance.

Figure 5.8 A member in the process of surveying the Cathedral at Ealing Grove. Note the bell in his right hand and the lota in his left. Barbados, 2009. (Photo by Felix Kerr.)

One notable observation was that the Church members were almost all barefooted, a reminder that Spiritual Baptists do not wear shoes on hallowed ground. When I first visited the Church in the early 1980s, this rule was practically immutable. Over twenty-five years later, I have observed that some women wear a soft closed or open pair of slippers in the Church. I have also noted that outsiders are often attending funerals and weddings at the Church, and they are not asked to remove their shoes.

With the guards in place, the congregation sang the usual doxology hymn, "Praise God from whom all blessings flow", while two women rang the hand bells. They then proceeded to survey the Church, with a bell in the right hand and a lota in the left. They went first to the main entrance, then to the first side entrance and to the second. Afterwards they completed the surveying by returning to the main entrance and to the low altar, or "people's altar". Throughout this activity, the congregation continued singing hymns.

A surprising sight was a woman who appeared to do her own surveying. She had her right arm extended and slightly elevated, with the hand seemingly curved around a container. But her hand was visibly empty. I inquired of a member whether the woman was indeed surveying and was told that she was carrying out that act. The member had seen the woman do it before and had concluded that the woman had been given this unique chore in a dream or vision. It was assumed that the Leader had approved this gift to the woman.

While the service was in progress, latecomers entered in full view of everyone and engaged in a ritual that I recalled was the formal way to enter a Spiritual Baptist Church. First, the person makes a salutation at the entrance to the Church by tapping the floor three times, representing Father, Son and Holy Ghost. He salutes the two guards at the door who represent angels guarding the sanctuary and then continues to the prayer-rail to offer himself to God by kneeling and praying there. Afterwards, the member gets up and offers himself to God and the altar by opening his arms three times in the name of the Trinity. He then greets the brethren in the Church by extending his right arm across his chest at the level of the heart, with the palm open and facing outward, and spinning around three times in clockwise fashion. Turning to the left is rarely encountered in Spiritual Baptist rituals.

Figure 5.9 Member surveying the Cathedral at Ealing Grove, holding a container not visible to the eye. Barbados, 2009. (Photo by Felix Kerr.)

After considerable hymn singing had occurred, the ceremony turned to Bible readings. The first one was taken from Job, followed by singing of the Gloria ("Glory be to the Father and to the Son"). The congregation always stands as they recite the Gloria, each member with the right arm raised into the air and the first finger extended. This act symbolizes the glorification of God. Then another hymn was sung, which was accompanied by more surveying of the Church. Following that, the Church went into what they call the "Pentecostal Prayer", during which everyone kneels and sings or speaks aloud the prayers that he or she wishes to offer up to God. It creates a peculiarly noisy atmosphere that stands in sharp contrast to the usual context encountered in many other churches where the congregation remains silent while one person, clergy or laity, leads the group in prayer. I have seen other Spiritual Baptist services where the traditional modality is operative, but this Pentecostal form of praying seems to allow the group to stand before God as a family and to have each member present individual entreaties for help and blessings. In the Friday night service that I observed, this phase of prayer was stopped when the minister leading the service moved into recitation of the Lord's Prayer, followed by the public and collective recitation of Psalm 23.

The congregation then sang another hymn while members walked around in the Church and greeted each other. These greetings were not done using the traditional handshake, as is commonly observed in other denominations. Rather, in this Church, individuals embraced each other without regard to gender and, starting on the right side, touched cheek to cheek three times, ending with the right side. Afterwards they sang "The church's one foundation is Jesus Christ her Lord", a well-known Protestant hymn that has become the Church's anthem and has been sung at every service I have attended. This hymn was apparently chosen by the Archbishop to represent unity of the Church and the connection of the saints within it to those in heaven. The hymn was accompanied by a resurveying of the Church and vigorous bell ringing.

At this point, the congregation returned to reading passages from the Bible. The first was read in unison by a group of young males, while a group of young females read the second passage. These group readings were followed by readings carried out by individuals – three males and three females. The passages were taken exclusively from the Old Testament, Psalms and Exodus, and seemed to have no clear, unifying theme. Once the readings were done, a collection was taken up.

While the collection was being taken, the young man who was at that point leading the service raised a number of different hymns and chants that varied in rhythm and mood. At this point, a newcomer to the Church would undoubtedly be struck by the contrast between the singing in a Spiritual Baptist Church and that in the traditional Protestant faiths found in Barbados. Spiritual Baptists sing the traditional hymns found in any Protestant service, as well as gospel songs and spirituals. Indeed, most of what they sing is found in the popular Sankey Hymn Book. A Trinidadian Spiritual Baptist group called the West Indian United Spiritual Baptist Sacred Order has also published a collection of hymns and choruses from which Spiritual Baptist churches commonly borrow their singing material.

The content of Spiritual Baptist hymns is not particularly unusual. At times, however, I have closed my eyes and focused on the rhythm of what was being sung and could find no difference from the rhythm of a calypso. In addition, Church members move to these rhythms exactly as any West Indian would ordinarily move to a calypso at carnival time. (I make no reference here to excessive forms of dance seen at carnival, such as movements that easily evoke sexual activity. I have never seen such obviously provocative behaviour in a Spiritual Baptist service. Spiritual Baptist dancing is expected to be in the service of glorifying God.) Furthermore, since, in this particular Church, fairly accomplished drummers regularly accompany the singing, the ambience in the Church may be transformed into a context that I know most Barbadians have never witnessed within the precincts of a church. On Palm Sunday in 2008, I attended the service at the Cathedral in Ealing Grove, Christ Church, which had 350 people in attendance at its high point. It was a special experience to hear that number of people singing hymns in the Spiritual Baptist mode.

In the Friday night service that I observed, the joyous singing continued for an extended period of time before the young man leading things quieted down the Church and called another minister to make announcements. Notices were given about coming services and also reminded members of those who were sick at home or in hospital. Another hymn was then sung and a special text was read, taken from Psalm 95:6.

The reading of the special text heralds the beginning of the time when short sermons are delivered by members of the Church. This is a variable part of the service that could change if the Archbishop is present, as he may dominate the service with his own preaching. But, in this case, his absence allowed matters to proceed in the following way: nine individuals were invited by the moderator to come and deliver some words to the congregation. As the speakers left the pew for the pulpit or lectern, they each raised a hymn that was expected to reflect their spiritual moods that night. Four men and five women spoke. No homily was really linked to the text that had preceded the preaching. The Bishop began the round of homilies, followed by an Abbess.

I was surprised only by one of the preachers. He returned to the theme of a disagreement that had been polarizing the Church for the last few months. I was taken aback because I thought that, with the Archbishop's obvious absence, there was no need to reopen sores that had been so troublesome. I learned after the service that some people believed that the reopening of the topic was meant to gain favour with the Leader. Hence, the speaker's motivation evoked more suspicion than I am sure he wanted. His expressed support for the Archbishop did little to settle down the dispute. In addition, following the mini-sermons, someone raised the civil rights hymn "We shall overcome", which was sung a bit tepidly. The ambivalence in the lukewarm singing suggested that members were not sure who was supposed to be the underdog trying to overcome oppressive dominance. The disagreement was not over, and neither side was giving ground yet.

The Church was then darkened as the final altar call was made. A reverend pronounced the benediction, and a final hymn was sung. Five women rang bells together, and surveying of the Church was done for the final time that night, while a number of other women formed lines at the main entrance to the edifice. In unison the congregation recited, "We thank you, Lord, for this our spiritual food, but most because of Jesus' name. Let manna to our soul be given; the bread of life came down from Heaven. For Christ's sake, Amen."

A minister then said, "Jesus be with thee."

The members responded, "And with thy spirit."

And a minister gave a blessing that ended the service.

SERVICES AND OTHER SACRAMENTAL RITUALS

The Sunday service generally follows the outline of the Friday night service. Variations in ritual occur for several reasons, however. First, services on Sunday last much longer, especially when the Leader is present. If he is not there, services are limited to three hours. I have seen services directed by him on a Sunday that ran between six and ten hours. Second, Sunday services may incorporate other rituals, such as a christening or a wedding. Third, Spiritual Baptists routinely state that the Holy Spirit influences individuals during a service, which may account for the Leader's decision to prolong a certain aspect of the service. This prolongation is then explained as the will of the Lord. Spiritual Baptists see nothing paradoxical or contradictory about the fact that, when the Leader is not present, the service must end on time, but when he is present, the Spirit may move to prolong the service. The Sunday service takes place at the Ealing Grove Cathedral and starts at nine in the morning. Some years ago, it started at three o'clock in the afternoon and went late into the evening.

I have raised many questions about the length of services and about the imprecision of starting and finishing times, as it seems to me that the lack of clarity about this feature of Barbados Spiritual Baptist services might create difficulties for the family life of members. Children find it hard to concentrate on the services when they are so long, and the youngest among them are sometimes seen sleeping under the pews. I have often wondered whether services could be shortened and other activities devised to occupy the members' interests and allow them to focus on important dimensions of their secular lives. For example, the young could be helped to sharpen their skills in reading and writing, adults could be taught about health and nutrition matters or they could be brought together to discuss fundamental subjects such as the history and beliefs of their own faith.

My discussions with a theologian from another Barbadian faith put the subject of unusually long services into a different perspective. He suggested that the Spiritual Baptist service should be seen as a community "happening" that melds the secular and the sacred and evokes an African sense of community. In addition, if contemplated in a context of restricted financial resources, those who attend such services don't have the problem of figuring out how to use their time on Sundays, which is therefore a blessing and not a problem. He argued that the distinction between sacred and secular was a European idea that caused havoc among the African slaves and their descendants.

In observing many Sunday services over time, I have noticed a striking feature: the Leader often introduces some mechanism into the service to make services different and unusual. Sometimes, these opportunities present themselves naturally – for example, a christening may occur. This, in itself, is of interest to the members, as even a simple christening presents the opportunity for members to talk about the baby's family and related matters. The same thing applied to a wedding I witnessed. People talked about the newlyweds with a vigorous sense of scrutiny. On another Sunday, the Leader used part of the service to bless new garments that were given to certain members. Since no member can wear a new garment without the approval and liturgical blessing of the Archbishop, the ritual is important. And since the new garment's colour and the seals it bears will have precise meaning to its owner, the provision of new garments is always of some interest to members of the congregation.

The unpredictable length of the Sunday service clearly provides the opportunity for the Leader to develop more complex rituals for Sunday than would be found in a weekday service. So, for example, the manner of closing the Sunday service is organized with more military precision. In this ritual, one woman stands in the middle of the Cathedral while other women stand at each of the four corners of the Church. The woman in the centre rings her bell seven times. This action is answered by the other four women, who each provide seven corresponding rings. The five women then meet in the centre and ring three strokes in unison. A hymn is sung by the congregation. As the service ends, the congregation stands up facing the altar, with their arms folded across their chests. Everyone completes a turn once to the right in a sign of peace. The guards from the three doors of the Cathedral approach the centre, offer prayers and move to return their tools to the storage place, led by the bearer of the shepherd's rod. A hymn is then sung, and the service comes to an end.

The idea has struck me, of course, that in the olden days it would have been difficult for Spiritual Baptist leaders to implement such rituals, because they would have been preoccupied with avoiding any formalized rituals that drew attention to their prohibited services. Their churches were certainly small and consequently did not encourage the development of rituals that would have required space to enhance their aesthetic appeal. Furthermore, church membership would have been too small for so many people to participate in a single aspect of the service.

Barbados Spiritual Baptists do have the ceremony of the Holy Eucharist, and Holy Communion is taken in the form of red wine and a wafer. All members of the Church may partake. Before participating, however, each person is expected to wash his hands ceremonially in a basin of water located at the main entrance to the Church. The bread and wine are found on a table placed in the area of the centre-pole and one serves one's self. Neither bread nor wine is offered by a clergy member. The wine is provided in a communal glass chalice or in small, individual cups that are disposed of once used. The Leader emphasized in several services I attended that to be balanced in one's Christian life one must participate in the Holy Eucharist. I have learned of no ritual,

Figure 5.10 Table prepared for Holy Communion at Spiritual Baptist Cathedral. Barbados, 2008.

Figure 5.11 Wooden cart used to store wine and wafers used in Holy Communion. Barbados, 2008.

approximating confirmation in the Anglican Church, that is required of Spiritual Baptists before they may take Holy Communion.

Christenings, weddings and funerals are now routine matters for the Barbados Spiritual Baptists. The Archbishop has explained to me that, shortly after his arrival in Barbados, he sought to register as a minister of religion with the appropriate authorities, and his request was approved. This was in 1957, and he had just come from Trinidad, where Spiritual Baptists had been granted permission to operate lawfully a few years earlier in 1951. It is likely, then, that, before this point, Spiritual Baptists had no rituals of their own for acts that had implications both spiritual and governmental. I was therefore not surprised to hear the usual "Dearly beloved, we are gathered here together in the sight of God" being intoned at a Spiritual Baptist wedding. Much of the ceremony followed classic Anglican ritual that I had learned as a boy chorister in the Anglican Cathedral.

The christening was a similar experience, although the Archbishop had obviously added a number of flourishes I'd never seen before. At one point in the ceremony, he held the baby under its armpits and allowed its feet to touch the ground three times. Then, after turning to face each of the four corners of the Church, he raised the baby above his head before passing it to other senior members of the Church, who repeated some of these same actions. It appeared that the baby was being presented to the community of the Church, in addition to the four spiritual corners of the edifice.

The funeral services I witnessed seemed to have incorporated Spiritual Baptist elements as well as traditional Protestant rituals. For example, the coffin was blessed with holy water from a brass handheld tool I'd seen before in many churches. But then the lota and bell were brought into use at numerous points in the service. At the actual interment, after the coffin had been covered up, young children were passed over the grave from a male assistant to the Leader, then handed back to the relatives. I learned that this mechanism assured that the children's sleep would not be disturbed at night by the spirit of the deceased. I did not determine the origin of this ritual, although I am confident that it was not a part of funerals in Barbados in the early 1950s. I was a member of the choir in the principal cemetery of the island and had never seen this act before. I have wondered whether it has an African origin. It certainly suggests that there is credence attributed to the notion that the spirits of dead people can return and "pull the feet" of the living, something I heard in my childhood days.

Worth mention is the unique service conducted by the Barbados Spiritual Baptists on Good Friday. Many other denominations conduct a three-hour service that marks the suffering and crucifixion of Jesus Christ. The Stations of the Cross usually are observed in many churches, and are often marked by the recitation of prayers and the reading of scriptural passages from different points in the church. The Barbados Spiritual Baptists, however, have for many years raised this activity to a wholly different level, which has in turn promoted their visibility and prompted Christians around the island to think about them in spiritual terms.

The service begins at the smaller Church in Richmond Gap. The group then takes to the road and walks through many different villages and districts that border Bridgetown, the capital of the island country. Several hundred members attend, dressed in simple white robes for the most part. They can be heard hundreds of yards away, announced by their singing and the repetitive ringing of hand bells. Some women carry lotas, which they use to bless intersections crossed by the parading group. They stop at areas that represent a station of the cross. At this point, prayers are said, lessons read, and a designated preacher delivers a short sermon. Certain ministers glorify the station by writing seals on the ground just before the group moves on. Stops are also chosen to accommodate eating and drinking, as the pilgrimage takes several hours, sometimes as many as twelve. The group is proud of their established tradition of conducting prayer stations in underprivileged areas of the island and their commitment to enduring some suffering in commemoration of what Jesus did for them as sinners. The debate about the degree of African influence on these rituals continues in the field (see, for example, Glazier 1996; Mulrain 2001).

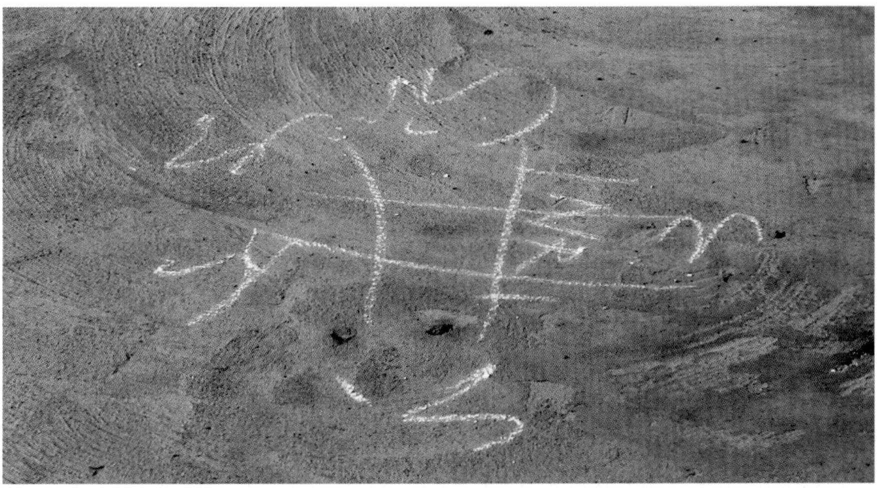

Figure 5.12 Example of seals written on the ground during the Good Friday pilgrimage. Readily visible are INRI (Jesus of Nazareth, King of the Jews) and Jacob's ladder. Barbados, 2007.

THE MOURNING CEREMONY

This ceremony has been of profound significance in the historical development of the Spiritual Baptist faith in Barbados over the last fifty years. It was not a part of the Barbados Church's ceremonies in the initial stages of the Church's development, as the Leader had not yet received the gift from the Holy Spirit that permitted him to lead a mourning service. Spiritual Baptists always caution that one must be approved by the Holy Spirit in order to "put somebody down to mourn". The Leader eventually received the authority from the Holy Spirit, and it was approved by his spiritual father in Trinidad, Archbishop Griffith.

In mourning, individuals are placed in some isolated part of the church, with eyes and ears banded so that they receive minimal or no auditory and visual stimuli. In the Barbados Cathedral, the mourning room is located in an area located behind the high altar and separated from the sanctuary where services are usually conducted. I have seen no other mourning room of such proportions, large enough to accommodate over thirty mourners at a time. While I have seen the mourning room in the Cathedral at Ealing Grove, I have never been there while individuals were in mourning. The expression "mourning ground" does not aptly describe the space at Ealing Grove, which is carpeted. But many years ago I visited the mourning area of a small Spiritual Baptist church on another island and was surprised that the mourning room, while enclosed, had a floor that was natural earth. This brought to mind the expression of "putting down someone to mourn on the mourning ground", and I thought of the word "ground" as we used to use it well over a half-century ago, as in "ground provisions" or "hoeing the ground". These terms were meant to translate dealing directly with raw earth, and I could see then why people mourning years ago were said to be on the "mourning ground".

There is much ritual and ceremony that accompany the mourning service, as Griffith and colleagues (1984, 1986) have described. They note that members have a number of different reasons for mourning, including a desire for spiritual strength and closeness to God; reception of a vision indicating that the member should go to mourn; a specific recommendation from the Leader; a wish to be healed from some ailment; simple curiosity; a wish for clarification of a spiritual experience; and a desire for advancement through the Church hierarchy.

Individuals going to mourn are first ceremonially washed and then anointed with holy oil. This process is called "purification and sanctification" and recalls what Moses did to Aaron and his sons, as described in Leviticus 8. Then the foreheads of the mourners are sealed by the Leader, an act described in Revelation 7:3–4. The Leader gives each mourner a secret password as a means of protection for them to use during their spiritual journeys. Spiritual Baptists give as a common example of a password the response Jesus gave as He was being tempted by the devil in the wilderness: "Get thee behind me, Satan." The password is meant to be used precisely in circumstances of fear or temptation, or to facilitate entrance to some blocked chamber or place during one's travels.

Before being put in the mourning room, individuals are banded. Broad pieces of cloth are placed over the eyes and ears to reduce visual and auditory stimulation. Banding is biblically sanctioned by Ezekiel 4:8, say the Spiritual Baptists. And the colours of the bands are determined by the Leader. Each band has its own significance, as is to be expected. So a red band, for example, is seen by some to stand for St Michael. Others prefer to see its significance in its being the symbol for victory or the blood of Christ. Banding has its own modern-day importance, as the reduction of sensory stimulation may

Figure 5.13 Bands used in mourning. Barbados, c. 1982.

contribute to facilitating entrance of the mourning individual into a trance. Once banded, the mourner is made to lie down in the mourning room or secret chamber. One may lie squarely on one's back or on the right side, but not on the left side. I have seen the head of the mourner placed on a Bible, which is thought to facilitate the arrival of visions and the dreaming process. Mourners are attended in the mourning room by specially selected mothers and nurses of the Church. The attendants appreciate the profound sacredness of the ritual and its long historical significance.

The act of mourning is sanctioned biblically (see Daniel 10), and the fundamental objective is for the mourner (Barbadian pronunciation often puts the accent on the second syllable with an inflection added) to have dreams and visions during this spiritual pilgrimage. Not every mourner succeeds in having dreams or visions, but informants uniformly agree that there is substantial social pressure on those who mourn to have that experience. The mourning experience of moving around in the spiritual world in a dream or vision is called "travelling", or the mourner is said to be on a journey or pilgrimage.

On returning from the mourning ground, each mourner recounts in front of the whole congregation what he has seen. The Leader will interpret the dreams and visions for the mourner at a later time in a private meeting. Through the Leader's interpretation the mourner learns whether his spiritual travels have been deep enough to merit his moving to another administrative and spiritual level in the Church. This practice may be seen as advancement on the ecclesiastical ladder through the use of spiritual criteria. Some observers are suspicious of a process that places so much power and influence in the hands of the Leader. But this has been the Spiritual Baptist practice for many years. It is also through mourning that members receive new garments, which also must be approved by the Leader.

Individuals generally mourn in multiples of seven days. The services that I have witnessed have started late on Saturday night, and the mourners return in a week on the next Sunday evening. When mourners are isolated in the mourning room, they are attended by mothers and nurses who are the only members, besides the Leader, permitted in the mourning room at that time. Much has been made of this secrecy by outsiders, who have claimed that it cloaks unacceptable behaviours that occur in the mourning room. My informants, including those who have left the Church and have no particular affection for the Leader, have assured me that they have never seen lascivious behaviour of any kind taking place in the mourning room. The fantastic stories that come from outsiders have often provoked my laughter, as these tales usually reflect profound ignorance of the mourning ritual and of the architectural configuration of the room that mourners occupy.

Figure 5.14 Inside the mourning room, showing spaces allocated to mourners. Spiritual Baptist Cathedral of Barbados, c. 1982.

The mourning ceremony also provoked suspicion in its early years from government officials on the two islands that outlawed Spiritual Baptist practices. I have heard that, in those days, mourners were put in isolation in coffins. The use of coffins in mourning has raised questions about whether the ritual was partly borrowed from Freemasonry, as perhaps were the password and some of the obvious symbols, such as the square and compass. In the past the time of the ceremony was kept secret – not the day, but the time. In Barbados, on the Saturday identified as the day for mourning to begin, members would gather at the Church, but no one knew what time the ceremony would start. The Leader made it clear that the time would be dictated by the Holy Spirit, and members would have to decide whether they intended to be there to support the mourners. Food was provided to sustain members during the long hours of waiting and, from my observations, it appears that the Spiritual Baptist community had successfully melded sacred and secular. Time was irrelevant. Mourning was a spiritual event shared by the community and mourners would be supported as they travelled to confront spirits from the other world – the reason why the password or key was necessary. It was just as likely for mourners to meet Satan as it was for them to encounter the Archangel Gabriel. The task was to emerge victorious in the spirit, more confident of one's connection to God and aware of what was possible in the secular world because of one's being grounded in the spiritual world.

Scholars have noted (Simpson 1966; Ward and Beaubrun 1979; Griffith and Mahy 1984; Griffith, Mahy and Young 1986) a number of important by-products of mourning, including the acquisition of advanced roles and titles within the Spiritual Baptist hierarchy, status and prestige, and permission to wear certain garments. Some attention has also been focused on the therapeutic impact of the mourning experience, as mourners often report feeling better after leaving the mourning ground, and describe an improved capacity to interact with the secular world. But, in my observations over the last twenty-five years, I have noted two elements that I believe now stand out in my reflections on the mourning ritual. First, mourners now talk with more emphasis on the experience of travelling in the spiritual world. They seem more informed of the functions of visions and dreams and the related utility of passwords or keys than mourners of the past. Those who mourn appear more invested in being able to live a part, albeit only a fraction, of their lives in the world inhabited by spirits. The second element is related to the observation that many members in the Church now own several different types of garments. These garments are obtained through the dictates of the Holy Spirit in dreams and visions, and members' experiences in acquiring the new garments appear most reliable if they have been had on the mourning ground.

CONTENT OF SERMONS

I will now describe the content of two sermons that I heard the Archbishop deliver. I do so because I believe that they provide illustrative examples of Spiritual Baptist beliefs. The first address took place at a funeral service in 2008 at the Spiritual Baptist Cathedral in Ealing Grove, Christ Church. In it, the Archbishop explained that the funeral service is important since it marks the passing of someone from this world to the next. He pointed out that death is just a part of living and stressed that, while some people think that death marks the end of life, that is not true. Death is not the end of anyone. It is passing over the sea that divides here from there, that separates the heavenly land from ours.

In the course of his sermon, the Archbishop pointed out that the best teacher spoke of everlasting life, and he cited the biblical quotation, "He that believeth in me shall never die" (John 3:16). He noted that life continues after death and gave as an example the case of Adam, who is, he said, alive and well. He also pointed to the cases of all the prophets who are said to be alive and well, and declared that the wicked too are alive, though not well. He emphasized that Jesus himself said that He would not die. Jesus withstood all the tortures inflicted on Him as a man, and asked his Father to have mercy on humans. The Leader argued that no one can kill a man, although one can stop his body from living here on earth. Consequently, there is no death, because there is everlasting life, and he reemphasized that we are all just strangers passing through. The people who love God and do good will go home to the eternal home in the heavens, but flesh and blood cannot enter the Kingdom of Heaven. That is why we have to put down the body. Ultimately, there is a gulf between paradise and hell.

The corruptible body, the Leader asserted, will become incorruptible. And the glory of the resurrection is that the dead will be raised up. He then asked the family of the deceased whether the deceased had pleased them. Were that the case, he said, they should pray to join the departed. Continuing, he argued that there should be no sorrow on earth. The mortal must put down mortality. Dust will return to the earth, and the spirit will return to God. He closed his sermon with a hymn: "Jerusalem the golden, with milk and honey blest, / Beneath thy contemplation, sink heart and voice opprest. / I know not, oh, I know not, what joys await us there, / What radiancy of glory, what bliss beyond compare." This first stanza of the popular Protestant hymn obviously underlines the message that the heavenly Jerusalem awaits those who have lived the Christian life here on earth. But the Spiritual Baptists often speak of this Jerusalem in literal terms, and many of them claim to have seen it in their visions.

I witnessed the second sermon at a Spiritual Baptist Church in Brooklyn, New York, that was founded by Barbadians who had migrated from Barbados to New York City. The Archbishop was in what I like to call one of his "political black" moods that day. He was emphasizing blackness in his usual tendency to claim that Christians in the colonial era hid much of black people's history from them. (This assertion serves as a reminder of Chatfield's findings [1998], that Spiritual Baptists protest against this form of colonial white domination of Caribbean churches.) The Archbishop began with the notion that Moses was born in Egypt, which is located in Africa, and recalled the glorious time when black people ruled the world. He moved into high gear and stated baldly that skin complexion has black people confused and preoccupied with the subject. And with a delivery that suggested he was revealing an important secret, he intoned solemnly that Jesus was not white. And though he used the words "not white" that morning in his sermon, I have heard his followers make the claim with more ferocity, stating that Jesus was a black man.

I tried to place this claim in better perspective even as I wrote the above paragraph. I asked two members of a Pentecostal church what their belief was. Both explained patiently to me that Jesus was not black. They cut the distinction more finely and pointed out that he had olive skin, that he was definitely not white. As evidence, they cited the fact that Jesus was hidden in Egypt for two years to avoid being found by King Herod's agents. Had Jesus been white, they said, he would have been discovered. I assume that many other distinguished commentators have had much to say about this claim. In the scheme of Barbadian culture, the truth of the claim is now largely unimportant. It seems almost an accepted notion that Jesus, whatever he in fact was ethnically, did not look white. The Archbishop and his followers like to claim to have been among the first in Christian Barbados to have raised this question and to have sensitized the public to the point that the established churches in the 1950s were papering over the matter and keeping black Barbadians ignorant of these fundamental facts. Spiritual Baptists still congratulate themselves for having made this contribution to Barbadian church history.

CHAPTER 6

On Visions, Possession and Symbols

IN THIS CHAPTER, I shall continue exploring basic faith tenets of the Spiritual Baptists. This time, however, I shall pay particular attention to the special role of dreams and visions in the orthodoxy of Barbados Spiritual Baptists, as well as their profound belief in the power of the Holy Spirit. I shall also describe tools and symbols used in the Church and shall point out some unique architectural devices employed in the Church to reflect the creed of the faith group.

DREAMS AND VISIONS

I have tried, without convincing success, to establish a clear differentiation between the terms "dream" and "vision", words commonly used by Spiritual Baptists. I once thought it possible to make the distinction based on whether one was asleep when the experience occurred. In other words, we could agree that both terms apply to a sequence of images passing through a person's mind. But in a dream it occurs when the individual is asleep; in a vision, the person is awake. My informants, however, were rarely confident of their actual sleep state at the time of the experience, except in a few examples.

On occasion, an individual might provide, with some assurance, the parameters of an experience and give an account that leads to the conclusion that it was a vision and not a dream. For example, an informant recently described being very upset about a disagreement with another Church member. As he entered a car and tried to start it, the automobile began to shake all over. He then heard the words of a specific hymn emanating from the vehicle. He was unquestionably not asleep in this instance, and was confident that the hallucinatory dimensions of the experience were all the more troublesome to him because he was awake at the time. Other informants, however, regularly told me that they had their experiences when they were at home resting in the middle of the day, and they were not sure whether they had been dozing. In any case, there is a biblical verse (Daniel 4:5) in which King Nebuchadnezzar refers without distinction to dreams that make him afraid and visions in his head that trouble him. For our purposes as well, it seems useful to employ the two terms synonymously.

One of the earliest biblical encounters with dreams is the story of Joseph (Genesis 37), who, even as a young lad, is already the envy of his brothers because their father displays a clear preference for him. When Joseph reports to his brothers that he has dreamed that they were together binding sheaves in a field when their sheaves suddenly stood up and did obeisance to his, the brothers are upset by the dream's implication that they might be destined to be governed by Joseph. In this case, Joseph's dream is an example of things to come in the future, just as it is also an important representational element in the narrative of his family's dispute. It becomes a channel for significant emotional energy, as Joseph himself is obviously struggling with the envy his brothers display toward him, the power of which almost costs him his life in an act of familial homicide.

Daniel is another biblical figure important to the Spiritual Baptists in the domain of visions and dreams. At Daniel 9:21–22, Daniel is praying when he encounters the angel Gabriel in a vision. Gabriel appears in order to give Daniel "skill and understanding" so that he may appreciate more clearly things that will come to pass, as well as his own responsibilities to God. Gabriel appears and speaks at a time when Daniel is praying, and is thus presumably not asleep, a detail that could justify characterization of this particular experience as a vision.

Dreams and visions consequently occupy an important place in the beliefs and rituals of Spiritual Baptists, who are always quick to point out the biblical basis of these experiences. Connection with God through the medium of dreams and visions is important to them, and we shall see repeatedly that they rely on dreams and visions to solidify their spiritual development and demonstrate their closeness to God. At the same time, the Barbados Spiritual Baptists are repeatedly cautioned by their Leader not to rush to interpretations and not to talk willy-nilly with anyone about these experiences. It is always advisable to take dreams and visions to the Leader for discussion and interpretation before revealing them to others. Presumably, the Leader has seen that the biblical Joseph's talking about his dreams to his brothers only worsened their relationship and provoked increased jealousy.

At this point, I believe it is instructive to be mindful that the dreaming process has been of significant interest to medicine and psychiatry for a very long time. Current views, such as those presented by Fosshage (2007), suggest that dream mentation, or using the mind in dreaming, is a process that occurs during sleep to digest information and regulate emotion. Fosshage has noted that "the images are not chaotic or without logic but have their own sequential order that captures meaning" (214). He emphasizes that thinking while awake or asleep serves to organize information into memory that provides an overall adaptive function that includes the regulation of emotion. He explains, for example, that extensive research has demonstrated that one's dreaming increases when one is learning unfamiliar tasks or coping with traumatic experiences. Dreaming also continues efforts made while awake to resolve conflicts and solve problems. As an example, Fosshage points out that when we have insufficiently expressed anger while awake, we may set the matter right by expressing anger in our dreams. In a sense, this function of the dream process may be an attempt at what the author calls the "restoration of self-equilibrium", a mechanism that in turn serves to restore one's self-esteem. Fosshage (2007) also cautions that "dreams are often elusive and difficult to understand" because of several factors: individuals often have difficulty recalling everything about the dream, symbols in the dreams may be complex, it may be difficult to put dream thinking and awake thinking next to each other, and often the relationship between the dreamer and the dream-interpreter may not facilitate exploration and interpretation of the dream.

I believed it useful to digress here so as to remind us of the considerable research that has gone into efforts to understand the complex functioning of the dreaming process as a part of an individual's life. Dreaming is, in a powerful sense, restorative and contributes to the decrease of anxiety so that we may in fact sleep better, in addition to functioning better the next day. For those who are interested in further reading about the scholarship of dreams, I recommend other work by Fosshage (1983, 1997) and Palombo (1978).

I can easily imagine someone raising the objection that Leaders in the Spiritual Baptist faith are ill-prepared to interpret their members' dreams. Indeed, one may be even more concerned about the practice of some Church members to interpret their own dreams and to keep them secret from others, including the Leader. Alternatively, one may assume that some members embellish a dream here and there in order to increase or to diminish its impact on others who hear about it. It is easy to imagine this possibility, as dreams and visions are the mechanisms through which God expresses His instructions to His people. Of course, informants repeatedly pointed out to me that the purposeful distortion of dreams must be a rare occurrence, since only the really foolhardy would run the risk of trafficking with God in this way. They reasoned that, since no one can fool God, distorting dreams to gain advantages would be an inherently self-destructive act for which punishment must be faced sooner or later.

I have already noted that dreams and visions play a role in helping some individuals make a decision about their choice of a home church. Once an individual chooses membership in the Spiritual Baptist faith, his growth and advancement in the faith will be linked to dreams and visions he will experience during his time as a member. To assure that the dreams and visions are being correctly interpreted, the member will of necessity have to present them to the Leader. I emphasize once more that Spiritual Baptists believe that dreams and visions represent a reliable index of one's spirituality or closeness to God. Consequently, it should be evident that dreams and visions have the powerful potential to be therapeutic, to help individuals to feel better about themselves and also to confront daily anxieties effectively. In a technical sense, therefore, dreams and visions may be seen as mechanisms with healing capacities. As one grows and matures within the faith group, one is expected to acquire the spiritual experience to manipulate the dreams and visions so that they serve this therapeutic end more consistently. Dreams and visions, however, should be seen as only one dimension of the overall healing construct within the context of the Spiritual Baptist faith.

MANIFESTATIONS OF THE HOLY SPIRIT

I did not mention earlier that several people were "filled with the Holy Spirit" during the Friday and Sunday services. This is a hallowed tradition among

Spiritual Baptists, and it occurs regularly at practically every service. Members are quite specific in describing the experience as one in which a member is "in the Spirit" or "filled with the Holy Spirit" – that is, the individual is "under the influence of the Holy Spirit which had come upon him". They distinguish between a "spirit of error" and the "spirit of Truth". Spirits of error induce one to carry out evil acts, while the Spirit of Truth refers to the Holy Spirit.

Of course, "spirit possession" is a term that has been employed for years in the academic community and has long been the interest of cultural psychiatrists. The phenomenon has been described in many different cultures, both Christian and non-Christian (Griffith, English and Mayfield 1980; Walker 1972; Simpson 1980). I acknowledge that there exists substantial literature describing the phenomenon of spirit possession in these varying cultures, and Henry (2003) and Lum (2000) have reminded us recently of the phenomenon's existence in the English-speaking Caribbean, particularly in Trinidad, and in the context of the Orisha religion and the Spiritual Baptist faith. I wish to emphasize, however, that among Granville Williams's group in Barbados, the spirit possession to which they refer means the manifested presence of the Holy Spirit, part of the Trinity. It does not include any of the African Orishas. In the Barbados Spiritual Baptist group, females seem to be more adept than males at being in the spirit. It is clearly not exclusively practised by women, however. At the Friday night service described in chapter 5, women got in the spirit and started screaming and dancing vigorously. One woman began spinning with such intensity that Church nurses quickly moved into place to make sure she did not hurt herself or someone else. Another woman started writhing and contorting her body, causing nurses to station themselves near her as well. In contrast, another member stood apparently transfixed and mute, with both arms outstretched toward the ceiling. She held that position for minutes before she dropped her arms and then walked off toward the people's altar. Often when the Holy Spirit falls upon a member, the individual speaks in tongues, in a meta-language that is sometimes understood by those who claim the gift of interpretation. On other occasions, no one seems to comprehend what has been said, and the event is simply seen as an occasion when the Spirit has manifested its presence.

It would be misleading to suggest that the manifestation of the Holy Spirit in the Spiritual Baptist Church takes place only when the music is dramatically up-tempo. I witnessed a mesmerizing scene at a Sunday service in 2008, for example, when the music was at a calming rather than exhilarating timbre. In the midst of this service, the Archbishop asked for everyone to lie or sit down on the floor. He then proceeded to sing very slow and meditative hymns. The congregation followed him, often humming along so that the resulting sound was soothing, and the Leader sat and made sounds that I associated with birds in a forest. The music was calmingly reverential, peaceful and almost eerie, because I had never in my life witnessed such a scene in a church.

Then, all of a sudden, people began to get into the spirit. Most striking this time was a young man who literally howled and kept on talking and crying for a very long time. I could not understand what he was saying, but others seemed to be able to make sense of it and to appreciate that he was communicating with the many spirits that were in the sanctuary at the time. In other words, as the Holy Spirit descended on this young man, he was able to communicate with spirits from the biblical past. Several members told me after the service that those with spiritual ears to hear and spiritual eyes to see could feel the spirits moving among us. One member explained that it was a teaching session in which the Archbishop was welcoming back the spirits of yesteryear, partly to give solace to the family of a member who had died during the preceding week, as well as to provide comfort to members with relatives in the hospital. Another member pointed out that the Leader had taken the service to a depth so profound that heavenly members were encouraged to return and visit us. As expected, I asked what spirits had returned. From Church members' responses I learned that present in the Church had been the Holy Spirit, angels and spirits of the elders, including Moses and Elijah. One member explained that the experience recalled the moment of the Transfiguration (Matthew 17:1–3), when Jesus was on the mountain and Elijah and Moses were there. This experience made clear to me that the Spirit can manifest its presence in many ways in Spiritual Baptist belief, and the phenomenon can last seconds or for a more extended period, even a full hour. In addition, the Holy Spirit does not manifest its presence only in the "hot" periods of the service.

This episode was not quite over, even when I had concluded that it was done and the Church members were all spent emotionally and physically. The Archbishop kept masterful control of things through his manipulation of the musical ambience. He suddenly struck up a hymn with a soft, march-like rhythm. The drummers caught on and moved into a semi-military cadence, with the drums muffled. Then a woman walked in a clockwise direction under the open space in the centre of the Church that is called the centre-pole. She carried a lota in her right hand, with her arm extended above her head, and she moved with the utmost majesty, keeping perfect time with the rhythm of the drums.

As she moved in her circular performance, an Elder wearing a robe with a cape appeared and began his own freeform dance, producing indecipherable shapes as he raised and lowered the cape. He too kept time with the drums, even as the woman seemed totally unaware of his presence. But they complemented each other, creating a scene of indescribable beauty. It was the kind of moving event I believed would settle any doubts members had about the presence of the Holy Spirit. I have had this thought on occasion in other churches, when individuals present would talk about being moved to tears by the spiritual beauty and solemnity of what they were witnessing. But of course, such experiences are distinctly personal. What moves one person may have no effect at all on somebody else. Still, I was moved as I watched these two Spiritual Baptist members carry out their dance accompanied by drums, and with the congregation humming softly. The ritual was a strange mixture of Africa, Barbados and England. But the context was entirely Christian. I wondered whether I would ever witness something similar again.

I could not tell whether these two dancers were carrying out their performance under the influence of the Holy Spirit. Their dancing was perfectly controlled and linked to the drum pattern, with nothing at all frenzied about what they were doing. Furthermore, neither dancer emitted any sound at all, and no one else joined them in the space of the centre-pole. So it seemed that something special was happening, and the solemnity of the moment prevented other members from intervening or joining in this performance. I concluded that the group believed that the two dancers were in the spirit. And I could not tell whether they were in what students of these phenomena might call a trance state, since their behaviour was distinctly ordered and controlled. Pearl Primus (1993), the famous Afro-Cuban dancer and choreographer, has made reference to the significance of dance in the Barbados Spiritual Baptist ceremony. Indeed, dance and singing are two important areas ripe for exploration by those interested in Spiritual Baptist performative rituals.

During a Sunday service in 2009, a male Church member appeared to go into the spirit. He started shouting instructions at another minister in a loud voice, while walking around the church in a very agitated manner, gesticulating

Figure 6.1 A member worshipping in dance at the Ealing Grove Cathedral. Barbados, 2009. (Photo by Felix Kerr.)

a lot with his arms. I wondered whether there was a modicum of hostility in the minister's voice and behaviour. He certainly looked disturbed and anxious. Other members told me they didn't think so, and they were of the view that he was simply trying to transmit the Spirit's message to another member of the Church. I was unconvinced and thought that the Spirit might have found a more pleasant and less disturbing way to convey what was wanted, since the man's shouts certainly disturbed the service. But, of course, the counter to that was that nobody is ever in a position to second-guess how the Spirit works out its purpose. Nevertheless, I continued my inquiries about this episode and found other observers who were confident that this was not an occasion on which the Spirit had manifested its presence. They concluded that this individual had displayed a lot of passion, but not true spirituality, and that he seemed to be disturbing the service more than he was contributing to its spirituality.

Then a member said to me that the Holy Spirit does not sow confusion in

Figure 6.2 Group of women praising God in dance. Barbados, 2008.

a church. It was a simple but profound observation that left me thoughtful for a long while. I remembered that one of the Barbadian Pentecostal members I had interviewed told me that the Holy Spirit is a restraining power that provides wisdom so that anybody in the spirit knows when to open and when to shut his mouth. This informant pointed out that the Holy Spirit promotes decency and order and struggles against mass confusion in a church.

It was clear in my mind that I had no ready criteria to determine when someone was truly in the spirit. But other members of the Church suggested, nevertheless, that one has to manifest a certain dimension of positivity for the experience to be authentic. I felt sure, too, that this particular episode was being judged in light of the partisan bickering that was then permeating the organization. The result was that many episodes of this genre were being scrutinized, and the standard of authenticity, whatever it was and however it was usually defined, was higher than ever before.

In that same service, I witnessed another minor incident that demonstrated once more the diverse ways in which Spiritual Baptists believe the Holy Spirit makes its entrance. The Archbishop was walking in the centre aisle of the Church during the service, and he seemed to be leaving the sanctuary for an unknown reason. Suddenly a middle-aged woman approached and spoke to him. I immediately had the impression that she was from another church and wanted to greet him before she left the service. They greeted each other with the three-cheek embrace I have already described (see p. 70). But then, with her right hand in his, he spun her around, gently but with a whip-like action to his arm. She went into the spirit and started to look as though she was stumbling from one leg to the next. The Archbishop next clapped his hands, and she moved toward him. He touched her and then let her go, and she returned to her pew, visibly still dazed by the interaction. Afterward, the woman wore a look of contentment throughout the service. I concluded, without verifying it with her, that she was pleased by the interaction with the Archbishop. Their personal meeting had been blessed by the appearance of the Holy Spirit, which had in turn confirmed the Leader's standing as a man of God.

Over the years, I have discussed extensively with non-believers this phenomenon of being in the spirit. They usually pose a number of legitimate questions that may be at least partly answered. But the response is rarely completely satisfying to those who are outside the circle of the culture and that of the believers. In Barbados, falling in the spirit appears in many Christian rituals, including those of Baptists, Pentecostals, the Church of the Nazarene and others. Indeed, charismatic subgroups are said to be operating now among even the Anglicans and Catholics. These groups are also known to embrace the experience during which the Holy Spirit supposedly manifests its presence, and they point to Acts 2 as biblical proof of its Christian authenticity. As a result, very few people in Barbados criticize the Spiritual Baptists for their belief in going into the spirit.

Of course, the Holy Spirit is actually, according to Spiritual Baptists, just one of many spirits that may show their presence at one time or another. I have discovered from many informants outside the Church that this dimension of Spiritual Baptist beliefs may in fact be shared by a cross-section of other Christians, although they talk about it less clearly than do the Spiritual Baptists. For example, a Spiritual Baptist member approached me after a midweek service one evening and asked whether I recognized that a particular woman's spirit had been present in the Church that evening. It turned out that the woman referred to had died recently. Obviously, I inquired how the member knew of the spirit's presence. She replied as though she were providing instruction to a beginner in these matters and made clear that the deceased woman's perfume had obviously been in the air. But, in order to pick up on it, one needed to have one's senses attuned to the spiritual world, which explained why I missed the evidence altogether.

At another time, however, I did have the last word, at least in my own mind. After attending another evening service, a Church member came to me and explained that she was upset because a visiting member from another Caribbean island had left a handkerchief in the pew. My informant explained that she promptly drew the visitor's attention to the oversight and made sure that the visitor picked up the handkerchief and left with it. I was made to understand that such behaviour can't be allowed to go on in Barbados. It should be obvious that for a few seconds I didn't grasp the reason for my informant's concern. Then it dawned on me that my informant was referring to the old Barbadian fear of people from other islands who are reputed to be more familiar than Barbadians with the spirit world, including good and bad spirits. Presumably the visitor had been contemplating some form of spiritual mischief through the instrument of the handkerchief. I never did get the story straight about what might have happened, or what potentially momentous event I missed. I laughed as I quickly realized that this kind of heightened sensitivity to the spiritual dimension has good and bad aspects to it. If one is in equilibrium with the world of spirits, then one's mind is at ease. But the slightest disequilibrium may lead to a quick burst of anxiety or a more prolonged state of unease. I was unconcerned about the supposed machination linked to the handkerchief because I just couldn't see it. I didn't have the eyes to appreciate the possibility of the visitor's action. Indeed, to this day I still laugh about the experience, since I cannot ignore the distinct possibility that the visitor had simply dropped the handkerchief, something I do from time to time myself.

It may very well be my own bias that I find it easier to relate to spiritual experiences that reflect a therapeutic effect for those who are the participants in the experience. The event just described showed a sharp sense of suspicion and concern that evoked an anxious approach of the Church member to the visitor. Nobody felt better after the episode, which was also my conclusion in the Sunday morning situation that had a frightening man walking up and down the Church yelling.

In contrast, one Church member I interviewed described the experience of serving as a medium for the Holy Spirit in one service. This member went into a trance and felt captivated by an unseen force. He sensed that he was talking out loud and describing the different spirits he was encountering. He saw Adam, Jacob, Gabriel, Job, Daniel, Moses and then the Master Himself. The member found the experience absolutely real and he described it as a transforming encounter with the spirit world. It gave him a profoundly new vista onto what was possible in the depths of this faith called the Spiritual Baptist Church. He knew that there was a glow about his life then that was visible to other Christians, he felt renewed as a person and as a follower of Christ, and, above all, he felt better about himself. He was pleased that he had brought exalting messages to the Church, not debilitating words in his description of what he had seen. This therapeutic effect is clearly different from the dysfunctional impact of anxiety-inducing spirituality.

The concept of being in the spirit continues to intrigue anthropologists, psychiatrists, theologians and others, although they attend to this phenomenon under the general topic of spirit possession. Scholars are still pursuing various strands of inquiry as they seek to clarify this phenomenon that can be found in so many societies across the globe. Even I myself, at first blush, thought it obvious what I understood was occurring as I witnessed Spiritual Baptist members going into the spirit, and in my notes I termed it spirit possession. I was therefore surprised to learn that Spiritual Baptist members objected to this terminology. As a result, I decided to ask other Christians and proceeded to interview a Barbadian Pentecostal pastor about the concept. She too was fierce in her condemnation of the term "spirit possession" and refused to have it apply to the work of the Holy Spirit, invoking Acts 2 in all its transcendent solemnity. In her mind, spirit possession is applied to the work of evil spirits, and nothing else needed to be said. So both this Pentecostal Christian and my Spiritual Baptist members reject application of "spirit possession", a term used recently in the work of Cohen (2008), to the phenomenon taking place in their churches.

The Pentecostal minister went further in clarifying these ideas. She pointed out that the correct terminology is "being baptized in the Spirit", and explained that once we accept Jesus as our personal saviour, the Holy Spirit takes up residence in our minds. It is the Comforter, the replacement for Jesus, who left us to return to His Father. And it comes to guide us, to give us strength to stand boldly and proclaim His truth, to bear witness about what Jesus has done for us and about His promise to return. The entry of the Holy Spirit into our lives results in regeneration; one is made new and born again. Similarly, the pastor rejected Cohen's terminology of "executive possession" or "pathogenic possession". She insisted that Christians never renounce their free will even as the Holy Spirit comes into their lives; consequently, we never give up control of our executive functions. And the Holy Spirit is never manifested in illness, which negates the applicability of the term "pathogenic" to anything wrought by the Holy Spirit.

An important point in this pastor's argumentation is that one is always walking in the spirit. As took place on the day of Pentecost in Acts 2, however, a Christian may exhibit the power of the Holy Spirit through the mechanism of being baptized in the spirit, the external manifestation of which is speaking in tongues. She insisted that much of the other behaviour common among those "in the spirit", such as spinning and shaking, is very often just behaviour learned by Church members from their peers.

While Barbados Spiritual Baptists reject the term "possession", they nevertheless accept several descriptive characteristics advanced by Cohen and Barrett (2008) to define the phenomenon of being in the spirit. Individuals whom I interviewed agreed, for example, to the following: when an individual is in the spirit, that person's cognitive functions are replaced by the Holy Spirit; the Holy Spirit completely controls the individual's behaviour; the Holy Spirit is wholly responsible for the person's behaviour during the time that the person is in the spirit. These characteristics apply to the "Displacement Model" of spirit possession. The Pentecostal pastor, by contrast, rejected these elements, precisely because she noted that the presence of the Holy Spirit in one's life does not require any giving up of one's free will, although one may cede one's will to the control of the Holy Spirit.

In closing this section, I emphasize once again the potentially therapeutic dimension of being in the spirit. Coupled with the experience of having dreams and visions, it should be evident that the Spiritual Baptist faith, as practised by the Barbados group, has substantial potential to make adherents feel better about themselves and to feel better about functioning in mundane secular activities.

SYMBOLS AND TOOLS

The walls, ceilings and altars of Spiritual Baptist churches are often well decorated with many different symbols and also with tools that are used in rituals of the faith. I will give explanations here for a number of the symbols and tools commonly seen in the Barbados Churches, but this list is not exhaustive. I also repeat that leaders of churches may add to the list or subtract from it in ways that reflect their individual commitment to aesthetics and to their philosophy of the faith.

The lota is a brass vessel that represents the Church building. Its origin seems to be Indian, as indicated by any dictionary that describes it as a globe-shaped water pot used in India and usually made of brass. Many observers think that this tool entered the Trinidadian Spiritual Baptist Church as something borrowed from the Indian population in that island. When used ceremonially, the lota contains water, leaves from the croton plant and a lighted candle. The leaves represent members of the Church; the candle stands for Jesus Christ in the midst of the Church. The fire is the light of the world. The candle may also be seen as man: wax is the body, the wick is the Spirit, and the burning flame is man's soul. The water stands for purity. In surveying of the Church, water is spilled from the lota onto the floor in an act of purification. Outside the Caribbean, in places where the croton plant is not available, flowers may be used.

The cross is the symbol of salvation. It is a reminder both of the tree in the Garden of Eden, where man fell, and of the crucifixion, where man was saved. The vertical part of the cross connects heaven to earth. The horizontal part stands for the earthly plane on which mankind operates. The cross is at once the emblem of suffering and of shame, but it is also the symbol of hope.

The shepherd's rod is the sceptre of authority. It is the tool of the shepherd and the symbol of the pastor. In Church rituals, the curved rod is often placed around someone's neck in the symbolic act of pulling the person back to Christ. The rod may also be used as a seal and placed, for example, on a stole worn by a minister.

The hand bell is one of the most ubiquitous tools of the Spiritual Baptist faith. It is rung repeatedly in rituals as an act of praising God and to celebrate God's message. It also represents the gospel, the message of redemption. In calypso songs that imitate Spiritual Baptist activities, one can usually hear the ringing of bells. Bell ringing is also one of the activities that annoyed the authorities of yesteryear and led to outlawing of Spiritual Baptist worship.

The square and compass are known everywhere as symbols of the Freemasons. No one is sure how these tools entered Spiritual Baptist practices, where the square represents working to achieve perfection. It is commonly said that one "squares his behaviour" or "squares things" with God. The compass (in my grammar school days, teachers insisted on calling it a pair of compasses) permits one to draw a perfect circle. In that way we learn how to keep ourselves within the circle of perfection. Together, the two building tools permit the viewing of man as a work in progress, as man seeks God. As Spiritual Baptist symbols, the square and the compass are often shown as interlocking one with the other. Within the symbol of the square and compass can be frequently found the picture of an eye, which signifies the eye of God, who sees everything. The symbol of the eye is also found in Freemasonry, as is another tool used in Spiritual Baptist imagery: the set of scales. The scales are said to remind Spiritual Baptists that in weighing themselves, their lives must be balanced, always in equilibrium before God.

The Barbados Spiritual Baptists have adopted a particular symbol as the seal of their Church. It is made up of four interlocking symbols: a key, originally given to Peter, that opens the door to salvation; a sickle, a cutting tool with a short handle and a crescent-shaped blade used to reap the harvest and, by extension, bring in the harvest of souls; a cross and a shepherd's rod, both of which I have already described. The cross-keys represent the keys of Peter, who was given the keys to open and close heaven and hell – in other words, the keys to the kingdom of heaven.

One symbol that reappears frequently throughout the Spiritual Baptist faith is a circle with jagged edges at its circumference. Some see it as a sun; others view it as a wheel. The sun, which shines on the world, represents Jesus Christ, who is often called "the light of the world" in his power and authority. The wheel, also frequently seen as a physical tool, resembles a ship's wheel and reflects the notion that the Church is being steered. In addition to these symbols, a ladder is commonly seen on sidewalls and on the back wall of the altar. It recalls Jacob's ladder. Spiritual Baptists symbolically climb this ladder of perfection to reach the pinnacle of life.

Figure 6.3 Church member lighting the candle found in the middle of the lota. Next to it is the censer containing incense. Barbados, 2008.

Figure 6.4 Symbols on the wall behind the altar. Visible are the crossed keys, Jacob's ladder and the intersecting square and compass containing the all-seeing eye of God. Note also the different candelabra for three candles, seven candles and nine candles. Barbados, 2008.

Figure 6.5 The logo of the Barbados Spiritual Baptists. Key, cross, shepherd's rod and sickle. Above is the all-seeing eye. Barbados, 2008.

Figure 6.6 Symbol on the wall of the mourning room in the Cathedral at Ealing Grove, Christ Church. Note the reference to Ezekiel and the fiery wheel within a wheel. Note also the intersecting triangles as well as the skull and crossbones. Barbados, c. 1982.

Figure 6.7 Pulpit in the Cathedral at Ealing Grove, Christ Church. Note the wheel evoking the image of a ship, and the lion of Judah. Barbados, 2009. (Photo by Felix Kerr.)

RITUALS AND ARCHITECTURE

Many of the tools just mentioned, with others, can be found on Spiritual Baptist altars. In the Barbados Cathedral there are several altars. The ones most frequently used are the people's altar and the high altar. There are also two additional altars, one of which is located on either side of the high altar. Only the Archbishop and others clearly designated by him have the authority to perform rituals at the high altar. The people's altar is the centre of Church activity. It is there that surveying of the Church begins and there that lotas, bells, Bibles, candles and jars containing oil or other elements, such as water or salt, can be found. Also present may be a conch shell, which is usually blown at times during the service when everyone is rejoicing, and incense, which may be used in a censer or in the form of lighted sticks.

It is important not to extrapolate from architectural structures extant in Barbadian Churches to generalizations about what Spiritual Baptist churches in other locations may or should have. I have seen several Spiritual Baptist churches, for example, with only one altar, although this was principally because there was not enough space within the church to permit construction of more than a single altar. In addition, many churches do not have a large enough membership to justify the expense of building extra structures that will only find occasional use, or use by one person in the congregation.

The Barbados Church has a font used for christening. In the early days of Spiritual Baptist churches, the ministers had no authority to perform acts with legal significance. Consequently, they were not allowed to christen, marry or bury their members. In that case, there would not be a christening font.

Besides the altar, the most important structure in the Spiritual Baptist Church may be the centre-pole. Despite its profound importance in Spiritual Baptist rituals, it may in fact be the most difficult structure to describe, since the space or size and configuration of the church often dictates the structure of the centre-pole. Aesthetic developments and the financial status of the church may also influence the appearance of the centre-pole. In addition, informants have explained to me that not every leader of a church has been given a centre-pole by the Holy Spirit.

The centre-pole of the Barbados Cathedral is an elaborate structure that is rectangular in design and rises many feet into the air. This is possible because the ceiling of the Cathedral is very high. The structure resembles the type of

Figure 6.8 The people's altar and high altar in the Cathedral at Ealing Grove. Note the archbishop's throne and pulpit on the left. Barbados, 2009. (Photo by Felix Kerr.)

rectangular scaffolding often seen at interior construction sites. But other observers have told me that this centre-pole more accurately resembles a baldachin or baldachino, defined as a covering on four columns of marble or stone, or a canopy hanging over the high altar in some churches. The top of this centre-pole is crowned by one wheel placed inside another. The external wheel or outer circle bears twenty-four lights, and the inner wheel has twelve lights. I have not seen a similar centre-pole constructed in another church, perhaps because I have never seen another church with as much internal space available, both vertically and horizontally.

The smaller Church at Richmond Gap has cleverly melded its people's altar and its centre-pole. The resulting structure is semi-circular in appearance and rises about a foot off the floor. The notion of its being a centre-pole is suggested by its circularity and its presence in the middle of the Church. The altar function is obvious, as all the tools and other implements already described are located there. Branches of the Barbados Church located in New York and Massachusetts have no centre-poles, and centre-poles I have observed in other churches look quite different. I noted in a church located in New York, for example, that the centre-pole was arranged principally around a col-

Figure 6.9 The centre-pole and altar at the smaller church in Richmond Gap, St Michael. Note the many bells, lotas, candles and even conch shells, with the cross in the middle. Barbados, 2008.

lection of flags, with candles and plants playing secondary roles. In this particular church, which had a Trinidadian heritage, I was told that the flags were powerful representations of the spirits, and hence played a central role in Church ceremonies by their presence in the centre-pole area.

Editha Jacobs, an authority on Barbados culture and history, has suggested in an unpublished manuscript that the centre-pole may have African and European origins (2009). She points out that when Africans came in contact with Europeans in the late fifteenth century, African artists took note of the obelisk, a tall, four-sided stone structure that narrows as it rises towards a pyramidal top. The obelisk then took on meanings of power, as it was interpreted and developed by the Africans, and at one time apparently became associated with death and the resurgence of life. Jacobs posits that the obelisk has been transformed into different structures in the present-day Caribbean. In Haiti, it has become the Poteau-mitan or centre-post, which is the central area in Vodun ceremonies. Thus it is the principal link that ties together the sky, earth and underworld (where the spirits of Africa reside), and draws the spirits up to be present at the Vodun ceremony. Indeed, Jacobs reminds us that the Vodun liturgy commences with libations that start at the Poteau-mitan and radiate to other points of the structure, reminiscent of the surveying ritual carried out by Spiritual Baptists. In the Brazilian ritual of Candomble, the Poteau-mitan is said to be replaced by the Staff of Oranmiyan, a large pillar found in the main worshipping room. The staff extends upwards and stops at the ceiling. It is there that the most concentrated energy in the ritual is said to be present.

In Afro-Caribbean cults found in Jamaica (also referred to as Revivalist cults), Jacobs notes, there is found a white pole that runs from floor to ceiling, again symbolizing the connection between the invisible world of the spirits and Africa. Among her descriptions, Jacobs presents the tableau of a Spiritual Baptist church in Trinidad where was located a large central post that served as the centre-pole. The Archbishop of that church described his centre-pole as symbolizing the tree of life in the garden of Eden, a cross, Aaron's rod and

Figure 6.10 People's altar at the Cathedral at Ealing Grove, Christ Church. Note the many bells and lotas as well as the circular object at right recalling the biblical image of the fiery wheel. Barbados, 2008.

Figure 6.11 The centre-pole of the Cathedral at Ealing Grove, Christ Church. Note the resemblance to the Roman Catholic baldachin of old. Barbados, 2008.

Jacob's ladder. Another theory suggested by Jacobs is that the centre-pole may also represent the mast of a slave ship. This theory is based on accounts that suggest that, when African slaves were being transported to the New World, they were sometimes forced to dance on the upper deck of the transport ship in proximity to the ship's mast. Hence, the mast may have been seen as a mechanism connecting earth to the heavens.

The Barbados Archbishop describes the centre-pole as an essential structure in the Spiritual Baptist Church – the "navel of the Church". It is the area of the Church that attracts "spirit people", where spiritual people hang around. This central area belongs to "masters in the spirit". Nevertheless, it is evident that fiscal, architectural and other realities have made it so that the centre-pole has undergone mutations, a point also noted by Editha Jacobs. As I have already pointed out, some churches have no centre-pole; others have constructed diminutive versions, such as the one arrayed with flags that I mentioned above. There is also a new, portable version of the centre-pole.

SCHOOLS

From time to time, I have heard mention of schools within the Barbados Spiritual Baptist organization, although I have not seen references to schools in the academic literature. I found it difficult to obtain much information about this concept, perhaps because it remains one of the last bastions of Spiritual Baptist secrecy. I stumbled onto it one day when I asked an informant about the presence of the skull and crossbones symbol on an apron being worn by a member of the Church. I was told that the symbol usually indicates that the wearer is someone from the School of Ezekiel. At that point, I was told to read Ezekiel 37, where I found the prophecy of God's breathing life into dry bones. Hence, Ezekiel's children, as I once heard them called, have a special affinity for dealing with death and moving readily between here and the spirit world. It is also this special group that performs ritual ablutions on a corpse and prepares it for burial. The dreams of those in the Ezekiel school often centre on death and dying. I was given the impression that, from time to time, members of this school will improve their knowledge of things spiritual through talks and instruction from the Archbishop.

I was also told that other schools exist, such as those bearing the names of Jesus, Solomon, David, Jeremiah, Enoch and Melchizedek. I learned, not surprisingly, that those of the Solomon school knew many secrets and were adept at using seals unknown to many other Church members. This was in keeping with my understanding of the tradition that those working in Solomon's temple were aware of many secrets, which was necessary to protect those involved in constructing the temple. An informant explained how a female Church member had succeeded in penetrating the Solomon school, which was usually open only to males. The woman had a vision in which she was following a very secretive Church member. She was close enough to hear him use a password to gain entrance to a mountain. She did the same thing and found herself within Solomon's temple. She ran from room to room trying to hide, but was finally caught and taken before Solomon. He decided to allow her to stay but exacted a penalty, which was that she should lose a big toe. The woman was grateful for all that she learned about the temple. She reported, however, that on returning to the secular world, she sometimes had pain in the foot that lost the toe in the dream. The story accentuates the place of the schools in the Barbados Spiritual Baptist orthodoxy.

BARBADOS SPIRITUAL BAPTISTS AND SHANGO

Many descriptions of the Trinidad Spiritual Baptists (see, for example, Simpson 1980; Chatfield 1998) make references to Shango, a syncretistic cult that combines elements of Yoruba religion and Christian faiths and resembles Haitian Vodun and Cuban Santeria. Shango believers retain distinct rituals that evoke African divinities. As mentioned before, Henry (2003) has described the progressive socio-political legitimation of the Orisha faith in Trinidad. But, as we shall see, this contrasts sharply with the situation in Barbados.

The Archbishop in Barbados was consistent in his clarity about the belief system of his faith group. He preaches Christ crucified and has no truck at all with any non-Christian belief system; his singular reference text is the Holy Bible. He enjoyed regaling me with stories of his encounters with Shango adherents during the time that he lived in Trinidad. For example, he stated that a Shango queen once came to him to be baptized, and her Shango king was thoroughly annoyed by the Archbishop's haughty daring. The king apparently threatened to put a hex on him and cause his death if he went through with the baptism. The death was supposed to occur by drowning in the very water in which the baptism was to occur. The Archbishop went through with the baptism to demonstrate that his God could protect him from all that Shango could do.

None of this should be construed as a denial of the African influence in the rituals of the Barbados Spiritual Baptists. But the Archbishop is technically precise in always finding roots for his rituals in the Bible, or in establishing connections between what he does and God's demand that Spiritual Baptists live a Christ-centred life. For example, he could not explain solidly the origin of the square and compass used in his Church rituals. But he was quite relaxed in articulating that the square is a reminder of the command to square one's life with God, and that the compass should be used to remind one of putting one's self within the circle of Christian perfection. In other words, others might use these symbols for their own purposes, but he has labelled them as tools of the Christian trade, one focused constantly on the task of building a Christian life.

Having lived in Trinidad, the Archbishop has had first-hand experience with Shango. He also recognizes that people may seek to align spirits on their side to achieve malignant ends. He is never worried by this practice, however, because he conceives of the power of the Holy Spirit as beyond sophomoric attempts to harness spirits to control the environment. What worries him, I believe, is that inexperienced Christians in places like Barbados still have a fear of Obeah and Shango. This condition exists because many Barbadians have not yet acquired the strength of faith that can propel them to significant depths in the spiritual world. Put another way, they still don't know what is available to them in the true world of the Spiritual Baptists.

HEALING

Time and again I have encountered Spiritual Baptists' deep interest in the therapeutic dimensions of their faith. I recall, for example, the minor incidents I witnessed at the baptismal ceremony described in chapter 5, when members sought to avail themselves of the healing properties they attributed to the sea water that had been blessed for the baptism. I have also observed on several occasions Church members approaching the Archbishop during a service and entreating him to bless them by anointing them with oil. These encounters are often carried on in hushed tones so that the supplicants' requests are kept confidential.

In a scholarly inquiry carried out at an earlier time in the Church's history, Griffith and colleagues (Griffith and Mahy 1984; Griffith, Mahy and Young 1986) described different dimensions of healing in the mourning experience, some of which were passive and some active. In other words, some individuals went to mourn with the explicit objective of seeking a resolution to a problem; others felt better about themselves without specifically resolving particular concerns. In a more general sense, it seems clear that the mourning ceremony is helpful because it provides mechanisms for transforming one's life, both within the group and in the broader community. Obtaining robes for use within the group is a crucial experience for the modern-day Spiritual Baptist. The experience defines the person as someone unique and special. We should remember the woman who received the unusual blessing of being able to survey the Church with an invisible implement. This distinction deserves repeated mention as an unexpected mechanism for contributing to the uniqueness of an individual.

The role of healing in the Spiritual Baptist Church was also brought to light on one of my own recent research visits to the Church. After spending several hours chatting with the Archbishop and a few members, I finally left a small group who had stayed to chat with the Archbishop well after midnight. Among the group was a member who had waited patiently for his turn to bring his personal needs and concerns to the attention of the Archbishop. Of course, no one would discuss what he wanted, as everyone respected the confidentiality of his consultation. But the point of emphasis here is that the Archbishop serves as a consultant on matters of healing, which brings to mind the point made by Young and colleagues (Young and Griffith 1989; Young, Griffith and Williams 2003), that pastoral counselling is salient in the armamentarium of African-American clergy in community mental health.

Nevertheless, that aspect of the Church's roles and functions is not to be misunderstood. Indeed, I had earlier thought it useful to conceptualize the healing function of the Church through the mechanisms of mourning and other direct consultations between the Leader and Church members. I hope I have made clear so far, however, that such conceptualization is unduly narrow and inexact. Furthermore, it does not do justice to the complexity of the Church's beliefs and ritual activities, which work together in an interlocking matrix of mechanisms that lead ultimately to therapeutic ends for Church members. In addition, I have refurbished the way I theorize about the healing potential of this faith group, and I recognize better now that a good part of the Church's healing activity is centred squarely on psychological dimensions. As a result, I have garnered much testimony from Church members about how much better they felt about themselves, their enhanced capacity to make decisions in their secular lives, their increased confidence about how different crises in their lives would turn out, and their explicit pride in being members of the Spiritual Baptists. But these conclusions are linked to a wide spectrum of Church activities that supersede the mourning ritual or requests for personal health consultations with the Leader.

CHAPTER 7

On Spiritual Garments

ANYONE WITH EVEN A passing interest in the Barbados Spiritual Baptists would be curious about the garments that members wear to their Church services and would perhaps eventually be led, from an initial curiosity about Churchgoers' clothing, to pose questions about the manner in which the Church is organized as an institution. I believe that such questions would, at first, flow naturally from the recognition that Church members dress differently from members of other faith groups on the island. Spiritual Baptist Church members on their way to a Sunday service in Barbados are easily recognized by their robes and head-ties, which readily distinguish them from individuals going to an Anglican service, for example, who are usually attired in clothes worn for dressy secular occasions. Consequently, an observer unfamiliar with the Spiritual Baptist faith would probably ask whether the garments, given their uniqueness, have a particular meaning.

Further questioning by an astute observer would eventually lead him to learn that, unlike the members of most other churches in Barbados, members of the Spiritual Baptist faith carry titles, such as Deacon, Shepherd and Captain. It is in this context of difference from and contrast with other faith groups that I would here like to explore the Church's use of garments and, later on, its organizational structure. As we will certainly see, the two topics are intertwined in the Church, and it is hard to discuss one without referring to the other. But I shall try first to disentangle them so as to make the meaning of the various garments clear.

I initially used the word "vestments" in speaking to informants about the apparel worn by Church members, but I quickly realized that Church members seemed not to understand what I was talking about. They corrected me and employed the term "garments", which I thought was less honorific. I had no clear reason for reaching that conclusion other than that I have been influenced by my own familiarity with the term "vestments" through my Anglican background. But throughout this discussion, I shall adopt the term preferred by Barbados Spiritual Baptists, in deference to their custom.

GARMENTS IN THE EARLY CHURCH

From my interviews of several women who joined the Church soon after Granville Williams's return to Barbados in 1957, I learned that, after being baptized into membership, women in those early years wore a simple white dress "made just for Church". It was called "a uniform", and they wore it exclusively to Church services on Sundays. The dress reached below the knee by several inches, although it did not go as far as the ankle. It was gathered at the waist and remained plain, or the skirt might be pleated. For evening services on Tuesdays and Thursdays, women could wear a plain blue or pink dress that also became a "uniform" once it was exclusively assigned for Church wear.

In addition to the white uniform, women in those early years also wore "regalia" and cords. The term "regalia" refers to a type of sash draped over the right shoulder and tied at the left side of the waist. Everyone's regalia (used as a singular noun) was not the same. It could be blue, pink, yellow or red, for example, and the Leader decided on each individual's colour. It was also the Leader who indicated the colour of the cord (white, black or pink) to be worn around the waist of the uniform. One informant explained that, for Sunday services, she wore a white uniform, accompanied by pink regalia and a black cord. On her head, she wore a "three-corner head-tie", also known as the beginner's head-tie. Noting my obvious puzzlement at this description, she suggested that I imagine a square piece of white cloth. She then asked me to fold this imaginary cloth into a triangle so that I ended up with a point on either side and a point hanging down in the middle. The wearer could then take the two points at the sides and tie the cloth around her head. The middle point would automatically hang down in the back. For the weekday services, this informant wore a blue uniform, pink regalia and a black cord.

She explained that the black cord indicated that she had work to do in the Church. The specific type of work was expected to be made clear to her over the ensuing years in dreams and visions. The pink regalia meant that she belonged to the Indian School. Here the informant noted that there are other tribal schools, such as the Chinese, Arabian and African. At first, her references to "schools" were so concrete and specific that I wondered whether her terminology referred to secular schools. But then she made clear that these were only spiritual references. Church members went to these "schools" for spiritual instruction, which could only take place in the midst of a dream or vision. But, not surprisingly, she added complexity to the concept by stating that some members were "cross-breeds", meaning that they enjoyed more than one tribal membership. Indeed, I learned that "some people have passports to go into all these places".

From my inquiries, I also learned that, in the early years, males were baptized into membership and then given regalia, the colour of which also depended on a decision from Leader Williams. The regalia were worn over the clothes usually worn to church. Here it will be sufficient to note that, in the early years of the Barbados Church, baptized members wore simple garments to Church services. The men stayed in street clothes, with accessories added that distinguished them as Spiritual Baptists. The women, as described above, wore head-ties and Sunday uniforms that were recognized principally by their being white, but their regalia and cords would also make them stand out among a group of churchgoing folk in Barbados.

The reasons for the relative simplicity of garments and organization in the early years of the Church in Barbados were obviously multi-factorial. First, Leader Williams was likely inexperienced in dealing with Spiritual Baptist tenets in the context of Barbados. So he had to proceed cautiously. It is also said that, because he was starting out as the head of his own diocese, he lacked the spiritual experience and authority to deal with the matter of garments in more than a relatively elementary fashion. He may therefore not have been able to claim certain interpretations of visions having to do with garments and structure without the backing of his spiritual father. But Archbishop Griffith was in Trinidad, not in Barbados. Rumour also had it that Archbishop Griffith and Leader Williams were not in harmony about Williams's decision to return to Barbados. Consequently, Williams may have been hesitant to assert a certain authority in the initial stages of the movement. He pointed out, for example, that he waited for Griffith to approve mourning ceremonies in Barbados before going ahead with them. At the outset, Griffith was to travel to Barbados to lead the mourning ceremonies, but then decided against it and encouraged Williams to proceed. Finally, the economic situation in Barbados in the 1950s may not have facilitated the tailoring of multiple garments for Church, as they represented an additional expense for members who at that time lacked the resources to outfit themselves in multiple garments. We must also remember that, in the initial stages of the Church's life in Barbados, members did not enjoy the status of a faith group accepted fully by the broader community. Hence, both the Leader and members may have been hesitant to invest in garments that were complicated and drew attention to them in a dramatic fashion. But, as we shall see, things would change with the passage of time.

MODERN-DAY GARMENTS

I shall now turn to illustrating the various complex garments that have evolved over the years. I shall utilize examples to illustrate how individuals involved in the Church have been given both group garments and personal garments to wear. The examples are derived from the many stories I have heard through my interviews with Church members.

Group garments derive from membership in a particular group within the Church. Personal garments usually result from gifts received by a particular member through visions. But the Leader may also grant to a member the gift of a unique personal garment, which comes to the Leader through a vision. There are exceptions to these general rules, however. For example, I have been informed that a Church member may have a vision in which another member figures prominently while dressed in a particular garment. The Leader, on hearing the vision, may determine that the garment featured in the dream is authentically meant as a gift by the Holy Spirit to the member who wore it in the vision. As a general rule, it is expected that the Leader must give his approval for individuals to wear particular garments.

After many efforts at trying to understand the rules that dictate the wearing of garments, I concluded that the principal distinction governing the allocation of garments was between group and personal garments. Then several members pointed out to me that certain particular events may mandate what all Church members wear on a special occasion. They argued that there exists the category of Church garment, which can be seen as a group garment at the level of the overall collective. In the category of "Church garment" fall three robes: white, black and red. This categorization made sense to me as I witnessed the group assembled for the Good Friday procession that re-enacted the Stations of the Cross through several neighbourhoods. On that occasion, almost everyone was dressed in a white robe. But even then, some members wore other personal garments that set them off one from the other. For example, some wore leather belts with their robes or different forms of head-ties.

I once attended a funeral at the Church and noted attentively the garments worn by members on that day. I expected most of the men to wear a black robe; however, some wore black and others white, with a white surplice. Similarly, some wore a white stole and others used a mauve stole. The women seemed to be dressed in a more varied fashion: their robes were generally black or white, but their head-ties were white, black, black and white, or mauve. And still, even with the general theme of sobriety in the use of colours at the funeral, red on occasion still reared its head, and was made all the more striking because it was obviously discordant with the thematic tone of the ceremony. But informants explained to me that some members may not have had the money to buy all three basic robes. Or, on that particular day, a member may have felt that it was not in keeping with instructions being received from the Spirit to wear a black or white robe. Nevertheless, one could reasonably conclude that Church garments exist within the confines of a few unique categories, accompanied, of course, by the usual exceptions encountered in the Spiritual Baptist context.

What I will record here with respect to group and personal garments is not necessarily the way things may have been fifteen, twenty-five or thirty-five years ago. And certainly, present-day practices are not the same as what was done in the early years of the Barbados Church. I shall emphasize on more than one occasion that, fifty years ago, members of the Church did not have the money to spend on multiple garments. In addition, Leader Williams may not yet have had the spiritual authority to prescribe as many garments as he does today.

Many individuals first come in contact with the Barbados Sons of God Apostolic Spiritual Baptists while they are still young children. In a common scenario, parents (usually mothers) take the children to church regularly, as a reflection of their own commitments to the faith. In one example, a boy wore ordinary street clothing – what he described as "nice dress pants and a dress shirt", all neatly pressed – to Church well into his adolescent years. He wore no tie. He explained that, although he was not baptized, he still saw himself as a member of the Church. This meant that, in attending services, he sat with specific groups within the Church, usually alongside boys his own age. Despite his assiduous attendance at Church during a period of roughly fifteen years, he was attired in secular clothing and did not wear distinctive Spiritual Baptist garments.

In contrast, I found other youngsters who, following their parents' instructions, were baptized at the age of about seven or eight years. (In the context of Barbados, this is not unusual. Many youngsters of that age, in my generation, joined confirmation classes in their home churches.) Following baptism, they would be placed in the group of young boys called the "Sacred Hearts". The Leader granted them, as members of this group, a group garment that was worn only by Sacred Heart members: a plain white or red robe with twelve buttons down the front, with the buttons representing the twelve Apostles of Jesus. (I immediately asked whether Judas was included in the twelve and was clearly told that he was not. For Spiritual Baptists, the twelfth Apostle is Paul, who was named to the group after his conversion. I was made to understand that the eleven other Apostles had welcomed Mathias to their number, but Paul had been called by God. While this debate is not essential to our discussion of the garments, it is instructive to note that Spiritual Baptist garments play a significant role in the articulation of Church philosophy.)

In addition to this robe, Sacred Heart members wore a red or white sash around the waist, and regalia that varied in colour. The colour of the regalia for a specific person was determined by the Leader and could be white, brown, pink, yellow or cream. Some also wore a white surplice when carrying out certain activities in the Church.

Before making my inquiries, I thought it reasonable to conclude that members generally receive their first group garment at the point of their baptism into the fold of Spiritual Baptist Christians, an event that can take place while they are adults or children. In keeping with the recurring theme of exceptions, however, I was surprised to learn the following story. One member reported that he had a garment made for his son while the boy was still an infant. This informant explained that he had been influenced by a woman who returned from mourning and told the Church that little children should be put in garments for purposes of healing and protection. So he had the garment made for his son in an attempt to follow what he saw as a form of edict coming from the Holy Spirit, which was speaking through the woman. The man believed that what he did for his son was carried out for the boy's spiritual uplifting. The little boy's robe was white, with seven buttons down the front. Twelve would have been too many for an infant, so seven were used, which is considered "the perfect number". (The member also explained that "seven" was Jesus' number while He was on earth.) The robe was blessed and put on the child when he was christened.

My surprise at the creation of the garment for the little boy stemmed from my understanding that there is some uniformity about the way Church members think about garments. But as I have repeatedly demonstrated, Spiritual Baptist rules bend to the exceptions created by what members see as the working of the Holy Spirit. In this case, the member suggested that the Leader implicitly approve the robing of the infant for two good reasons: first, he was following his view that the Holy Spirit had intervened through the message of the woman who had just returned from mourning; second, he wished to protect his son from secular evil by the wearing of a robe, which was in keeping with Spiritual Baptist teachings about the functions of Church garments. Of course, the robing of the infant is also an example par excellence of Laitinen's (2002) idea of creolization within the Spiritual Baptist context. In other words, while following the bounded tradition of spiritual garments passed on from generation to generation, the Barbados Spiritual Baptist group can still find room to express creative and novel thinking.

In my many interviews of male Church members, I encountered the common occurrence of individuals' coming to baptism in late adolescence. For example, one member explained that he had strayed away from the Church when he was approaching the end of his adolescent years. His falling away from the Church was not a decision made after formal reflection and personal inquiry about what he intended to do concerning the relationship between himself and his Church. Rather, it just happened, under the press of activities at school and after school, and under the stress of having to make decisions about his future. He was also exploring different facets of Barbadian life which were external to the business of attending Church services several evenings a week in addition to the multi-hour commitment on Sundays. When he was a little older, however, he began to have visions with the repetitive theme of the world's coming to an end, with Judgement Day in process. In each vision it was clear to him that he had been caught unprepared for the return of the Master and the beginning of Judgement. These visions influenced him to consider life more seriously and to make a commitment to Christ. He then returned to Church and accepted baptism, after which he was taken to sit with the group called the Prince Shepherds and the Leader instructed him on the group garment that he should obtain. A few days afterwards, he went to give the order for his garments to a seamstress who was familiar with Spiritual Baptist attire. His first set of garments was made up of the following:

1. A regalia, with a cross on the front and a five-pointed star on the back. The cross represented Jesus Christ, so that, as the member walked in life, he would walk with Jesus Christ before him and man (the five-pointed star) behind him. As said before, different individuals wore regalia of different colours, as determined by the Leader.
2. A plain white robe with the usual twelve buttons on front.
3. A red cord worn around the waist like a belt.
4. A white surplice, which was to be worn when he was carrying out certain functions. (Prince Shepherds generally work on the altar or carry certain implements, such as the cross during processions. During such activity, he was expected to wear the surplice.)
5. A headband with a cross in the middle and two stars on each side of the cross.

He wore this garment as a member of the Prince Shepherd group for several years. Then the Leader, presumably on instructions from the Holy Spirit, decided to promote the group to be members of the Captains. This latter group has both male and female members, and they serve several roles. They work on the altar; some preach; others carry out a wider range of activities, reflecting their spiritual strength. Captains wear garments that suggest that they are "ranking officers within the body of the Church":

1. A white robe with twelve buttons on front. This time, however, the buttons were black with a gold trim and each had a ship's anchor on front. The anchor suggests fortification and stability, in the way an anchor provides stability for a ship. In this case, the Church is the ship.

2. A leather belt with a thinner leather strap attached to it. The strap fits over the right shoulder and is attached to the belt on the left side both in front and in back. These belts are strikingly similar to those worn by military officers in the British Army.
3. A biretta or turban to be worn as headgear.

He pointed out that the Captains have additional robes to wear on different occasions. The change is basically in the colour of the robe. A grey robe is worn at harvest festivals or other festive occasions in the Church. For a funeral, the robe is black; a red robe is worn at Easter and Pentecost Sunday. But, as usual, an individual may wear a robe of a particular colour at a given service if moved by the Spirit to do so.

In addition to group garments, baptized members of the Church may be authorized by the Leader to wear personal garments. One informant explained how he came by his personal garments through a vision. During this vision, he found himself in a cemetery watching a Spiritual Baptist procession at an interment ceremony. The Church members were, of course, attired in their garments, and he himself was wearing a pair of blue jeans and a blue shirt when a woman came out of Heaven and asked him, "Where are your clothes?" He replied, "I have no clothing. I am wearing the only clothing I have."

She responded, "You can't dress this way inside God's house." Then she told him to wait and she disappeared. She reappeared with a plastic bag in her hands and presented it to him, saying, "Ezekiel sent this for you."

He began to object and protest, and their interchange even turned into a physical struggle. But, all of a sudden, even in the face of his vigorous refusals, he found himself dressed in a Church garment. At the same time, the woman gave him the meaning of the garment, how and when to wear it, and the type of Church work to be carried out while wearing it. He received similar instructions concerning other garments that were also in the plastic bag. He pointed out that he could not divulge the instructions given to him, but he described two sets of personal garments he was given in the vision. For garment #1 he received:

1. A black robe. From the shoulder to the waist in back, however, the robe was white. And in the centre of the back in an off-white colour was the schema of a skull with crossbones underneath.
2. A black leather belt.

3. Three cords: a black and a red cord went from the right shoulder to the left side of the waist; a red cord went from the left shoulder to the right side of the waist.
4. A black biretta.

For garment #2, he received:

1. A black robe with red cuffs on the sleeves.
2. Six red cords to be worn around the waist.
3. A regalia made of plaited red cords.
4. Three black and red cords, to be worn around the shoulders in the same way as in the first garment.
5. A black biretta.

The next illustrative example is that of a female who joined the Church when she was in her mid-adolescent years as the decade of the 1960s was coming to a close. Her decision to join the Church was fuelled by an insistent mother. After about four weeks of sitting on the mercy seat, she was baptized by Leader Williams. She explained to me that her baptism took place in the northern parish of St Lucy, at a time when the Leader was regularly holding open-air services there – an historic reminder that, over the years, the Leader has carried out baptisms in the sea at different beaches around the island and even at different times of the day and night. Following her baptism, this member was assigned to a group called the League of Mary, whose work within the Church seemed quite fluid and nonspecific. Sometimes its members read a lesson or performed some other minor task within the Church. This group had group garments made up of a white robe, a cord worn around the waist, a regalia and the usual three-pointed head-tie worn by female beginners in the Church. The head-tie was also accompanied by a white band about an inch and a half broad, worn around the forehead and tied in back. As stated earlier, the colour of the cord and the regalia varied from one individual to another. As a result, it seems clear that even in the context of what I have been calling group garments, the regalia and cords actually reflect personalized dimensions. Thus, in examining the garments assigned to any specific group within the Church, it is evident that no group will have all its members in exactly the same garments, as the regalia at least will never be the same colour for all members in the group.

After spending about five years as a member of the League of Mary, this woman was promoted to the Teachers Association. This latter group took care of the altars and prepared the lotas. They also held candles while standing next to individuals who read lessons during the services. The Teachers' group garment was made up of the following:

1. A brown uniform. This term, as said before, is applied to a garment that stops just below the wearer's knees, in contrast to a robe that reaches the ankles.
2. A brown sash worn around the waist and dropped to the left side.
3. A brown head-tie, considered more advanced than the three-pointed head-tie. The head-tie at this level is made from a rectangular piece of cloth, with two long sides and two short sides. It is tied with a visible knot in the front.
4. Two cords: a red cord was worn from the right shoulder to the left side of the waist; a gold cord was worn from the left shoulder to the right side of the waist. Cords that cross each other in this way are called "lapcords".
5. A brown pleated apron worn in front and tied at the back. It is said to be a help in hiding one's spiritual nakedness.

With respect to this group garment, brown indicates maturity and red suggests strength. Gold is said to reflect spirituality.

The Teachers also wore an alternative group garment made up of a wine-coloured robe, a scarlet head-tie, a leather belt or blue sash to be tied around the waist and a ceremonial yellow and gold apron. Red and gold lapcords were worn, as described above. Wine and scarlet are said to denote royalty, and blue symbolizes holiness. Some members of the Teacher group are accorded the spiritual privilege of carrying a "pessy", which is a thin, circular, carved piece of wood about two feet in length. I have not been successful in learning the origin of the word or its correct spelling. But others have told me that the stick recalls the piece of wood used by elementary school teachers in years long gone by. One can imagine, from this context, that Spiritual Baptist Teachers could use the implement to explain matters or to draw diagrams.

After serving in the rank of Teacher for about twelve years, this Church member was promoted to the rank of Teacher Captain and remained in that position for about eighteen years. The functions in this senior rank are similar to those of a Teacher, but Captains can also participate in mourning ceremonies and in the blessing of garments. Teacher Captains wear the following group garment:

1. A grey box-pleated robe with shoulder epaulets and two breast pockets.
2. A brown, three-inch-wide cloth belt for the waist.
3. A gold and silver head-tie.
4. A pleated regalia, worn from the right shoulder to the left side of the waist, that can be red, green, blue, cream or black, as determined by the Leader.

Teacher Captains can also wear two other alternative group garments, the first of which entails:

1. A green pleated robe with epaulets and breast pockets.
2. A brown leather belt.
3. Green lapcords running from both shoulders.
4. A green cord attached to the right side of the belt and hanging down.
5. A green and gold head-tie.

The second alternative garment is made up of:

1. A khaki pleated robe with epaulets and pockets.
2. A leather belt.
3. Gold and red lapcords.
4. A bronze and gold head-tie.

For the last several years, this woman has been a member of the ministerial order. The first rank in this group is usually Deaconess or Deacon, and the Leader offered her an appointment to this rank some years ago. At the time the offer was made, the member did not accept it, as she believed she was not ready to take on the significant responsibility of this post. There were other things going on in her life that made it hard to concentrate fully on the duties required of someone in the ministerial order. But then, a few years later, the Leader made her another offer, this time to the rank of Reverend, which is a step above Deaconess. So, as Mother Reverend, she was allowed to bypass the rank of Deaconess. The Leader had measured her spiritually and found that she met the requirements for this position. It was explained to me that Mother Reverends are allowed to preach the gospel and to participate in many Church ceremonies, such as weddings and funerals.

It was natural for me to ask whether Reverends can function independently in carrying out their duties. I learned that almost all of them function in the name of the Leader and therefore are not registered with government authorities to perform certain Church ceremonies in their own names. I could not determine what made it difficult for the ministers to become independent. As a group, Mother Reverends may wear this garment:

1. A white or black robe with red inverted pleats on both sides and at the back, and with a minister's collar at the neck.
2. A black, four-inch leather belt for the waist.
3. A white surplice.
4. A white stole with a sickle imprinted on one end and a cross on the other.
5. A black biretta.

The examples I have given here for both males and females demonstrate the general principles of garment acquisition through two processes: promotion through the ranks of groups within the Church or, alternatively, through the intervention of the Holy Spirit by the mechanism of visions. But I have been made to understand clearly that garments are not distributed to a member just because that member had a vision about a garment. This point was brought home to me through a pungent Spiritual Baptist saying: "The dream may be true, but the time appointed may be long." In other words, a dream or vision may explicitly prescribe a garment for the member, but the spirituality of the garment may be too heavy a burden for the member at the time the vision is received. Consequently, the Leader may delay giving the member permission to obtain the garment.

So what happens if a member decides to wear a garment that has not been authorized by the Leader? One informant assured me that few members try to do that, as history has it that committing such a transgression can lead to a member's becoming mentally unstable. As evidence, another Church member recounted an event that he witnessed at a service. Apparently a member started to become anxious during the service and reported difficulty breathing, while tugging in an agitated fashion at the garments the member was wearing at the time. The Leader reportedly reminded the member that he had warned the individual not to wear those particular garments. Other members in the Church then proceeded to help the member shed the garments. Once that was done, the member found relief. Such stories confirm the general belief that obtaining garments is not a light-hearted matter. Just as wearing an approved garment may provide health, wearing one that does not properly belong to the wearer may turn out to be a detriment to the wearer's health.

In earlier days members might have certain garments taken off them while in Church. This apparently used to occur when someone in the Church had strong feelings that another member was not spiritually strong enough to wear a particular garment. The wearer was tested, so to speak, in front of the congregation, and if unable to respond in a way that demonstrated the rationale for wearing the particular garment, then the wearer had to give up the garment. In a sense, this was the members' attempt to safeguard the sacredness of their garments and the authenticity of the allocation process.

At the same time, however, it is easy to see why this manner of publicly embarrassing a member has lost its popularity. (I could not find informants who recalled its occurring to any Church members in recent years, although members did recall its happening to visitors from other Spiritual Baptist churches.) The practice certainly undermined the Leader's authority to approve the allocation of garments to particular members. In addition, it put everyone at risk of being challenged in a public setting, of having their garments and their authenticity subjected to questioning. Giving up one's garments in public must have been profoundly humiliating and would have been the subject of folktales within the group for years. At the same time, those disrobed must have borne grudges against their challengers for a long time, as I think it would be difficult to forgive those who had caused so public a loss of face.

The disrobing of members also flies in the face of one obvious role played by garments in the Spiritual Baptist faith: the fact that garments identify members as belonging to a distinctive group and bring members together in a unified way in opposition to all those outside that group. This was particularly true at times when the faith, and the Sons of God Apostolic Spiritual Baptist Church in particular, were still not accepted by the broader society. Hence, having one's garments and authenticity subjected to scrutiny by members of the group may have served to dilute the potential therapeutic effect of the garments. Some informants did explain that other Spiritual Baptist churches made it a rule that one could only obtain personal garments by going through the mourning process, which suggests use of another mechanism to safeguard the authenticity of the garment allocation process. The mourning experience makes it hard to question the authorization of garments, as it would force members to raise questions about the mourning experience, a privilege accorded principally to the Leader of a church. In addition, mourning has long been an historic, prestigious and sacred ceremonial tradition for Spiritual Baptists. It has also been considered to be the exclusive domain of the Holy Spirit and therefore beyond questioning by rank-and-file members.

I recognize that, in practice, it may not be easy for the average observer to determine a Church member's rank or group affiliation simply by looking at what the member is wearing. This is partly because members seem to prefer their personal garments to their group garments. Hence, the occasions on which a significant number of members will be seen in the same garment are relatively infrequent. Nevertheless, these occasions of homogeneity do exist. In my observations, the most obvious occasion has been funerals. The other event I witnessed that seemed to demand homogeneity took place when the Church was making a pilgrimage to another sister group. On such an occasion, Church members seemed to seek unity and identity in looking alike and appearing to make a sharp turnout.

GARMENTS AND THEIR ROLES

Members' garments play a number of roles in this Church. Not only do members believe that garments indicate the spiritual strength and faith history of each person in the Church, but garments also serve as documentation of a member's achievements and rewards. They also carry a message, which is enhanced by the way the wearer walks in the garment. The garments and the carriage of the wearer should project the spiritual seniority of the individual, who should always be uplifted by the garment. So, as one member explained it, a Bishop does not dress like a Deacon. The Bishop must look royal and superior to the Deacon, but not superior in the sense of being haughty or imperious. The garments must translate humility and spiritual depth, which for a Bishop should be perceptibly beyond that of a Deacon. This notion of spiritual seniority was important to many of the members I interviewed, just as it seemed important to many of them to have a way of distinguishing between, for example, a Deacon and a Reverend. But even so, the differences were not always self-evident. I also wondered whether evidence of seniority was most important to those who had it, and whether in fact members low on the totem pole preferred to wear their personal garments so as to hide direct evidence of where they ranked in the hierarchy.

Examples of group garments

Figure 7.1 Female member wearing the group garment of members of the Archbishop's Court. Barbados, 2009. (Photo by Felix Kerr.)

Figure 7.2 Member of Nurses' group: blue uniform with white collar and white edge on short sleeves; white pleated apron with SOJ (stars of Jordan); blue and white head-tie. Barbados, 2009.

Figure 7.3 Group of Teachers at a funeral service for a deceased Teacher. Robes are white with brown regalia and a white head-tie. Some belts are cloth, others leather. Barbados, 2008.

Examples of group garments (*cont'd*)

Figure 7.4 Classic white robe and white surplice of a Reverend, accompanied by a black biretta. Barbados, 2008.

Figure 7.5 Traditional black robe with slip-in collar and white surplice of a Reverend; with mauve stole. Barbados, 2008.

Figure 7.6 Woman in Deaconess garment: red robe with slip-in collar and belt; white shoulder apron; multi-coloured head-tie. Barbados, 2009.

Figure 7.7 Member from Captains' group; blue robe with leather belt and shoulder strap; matching blue turban. Barbados, 2009.

Examples of personal garments

Figure 7.8 Black robe with red buttons. Edge of sleeves and collar are also red. Cords are lapped and also used around waist and left to hang down. Barbados, 2008.

Figure 7.9 Cream robe with slip-in collar. White belt is cloth. Head-tie matches robe. Barbados, 2009.

Figure 7.10 Scarlet surplice worn over yellow robe. Turban matches surplice. Cord hangs around neck. Barbados, 2008.

Figure 7.11 Abbess in personal garment. Blue stole matches blue robe with slip-in collar. Chasuble is white and matches head-tie. Barbados, 2009.

Example of a church garment

Figure 7.12 Male wearing traditional blue work-robe with cross on back. Some people wear brown work-robes. Barbados, 2008.

Different forms of head-ties

Figure 7.13 Members dancing in the spirit during church service. Note the relative simplicity of the garments and head-ties. Barbados, c. 1982.

Figure 7.14 Member of the Archbishop's Court with a head-tie that is distinctive in colour, length and type of cloth used. Barbados, 2009.

Different forms of head-ties (*cont'd*)

Figure 7.15 Members at a baptismal service. Note the variation in head-ties. Barbados, 2008.

Figures 7.16 and 7.17 Pictures show a variety of head-ties worn in the Church. Differences are based on colour, length, method of tying and even gender. Barbados, 2007.

I have already mentioned the function of protection. Garments act as shields. They are armour, and in describing this function, members readily evoke Ephesians 6:11–12: "Put on the whole armour of God, that ye may be able to stand against the wiles of the devil. For we wrestle not against flesh and blood, but against principalities, against powers, against rulers of the darkness of this world, against spiritual wickedness in high places." These verses emphasize the role of protection in Church members' claims about their garments, but they also make clear that the protection is needed against spiritual forces that, in their own right, have substantial power. Church garments are yet another means of spiritual help, like passwords, seals, and personal hymns.

Garments are also a conduit for the Holy Spirit. In this regard, members have explained that, while wearing a specific garment, they have had unusual and striking spiritual experiences. For example, one member related how one day at Church, he was called to perform an act of healing on another member who was suffering from an ailment in one arm. The healer linked the urge to go and anoint the sick member to the powers of the garment. And from that day on, he has commonly had this feeling of the presence of the Holy Spirit while attired in that specific garment. Another member described how an unusual sensation of lightness, a pulsating desire to dance and praise God, and an almost irresistible urge to move come over him whenever he wears one specific garment among his collection. There is no doubt in his mind that these feelings represent the workings of the Holy Spirit. I must add that the presence of the Holy Spirit has also been described to me as having, in some cases, a direct healing effect on the wearer. So the garments not only facilitate curative acts by the wearers, they also may have a direct therapeutic effect on the wearers themselves.

One striking difference between the garments worn years ago and those of today is their aesthetic appeal. Members speak movingly of the beauty of today's head-ties, the obvious use of dramatic colour in the robes, the inclusion of saris and stoles and capes in the outfits. The evolution of the garments has turned into a veritable array of religious apparel that enhances each individual member and has moved Spiritual Baptist clothing into an arena ripe with the potential for competition. On the one hand, it is evident that the new style of garments makes members feel a profound sense of confidence in themselves as well as in their faith. On the other hand, members admit readily that the new garments sometimes evoke arrogance in themselves and envy in others.

Not everyone has the money to purchase all the garments to which they may be entitled, so having money is an advantage. In addition, some people have the physical attributes that allow them to carry off the visual effects of the garments with more ease than other members. This is why some older members naturally prefer the simple garments of yesteryear. Simplicity does not breed as much envy, and it serves to avoid the temptation of putting on a fashion show in the Church. These older folk point to the simple blue or brown cotton robes worn on Maundy Thursday, when the Church's hierarchy gather to wash the feet of the average members. This is the time when humility is at its peak and the Lenten season is drawing to a close, when spirituality is the order of the day and everyone is contemplating all that Jesus endured in order to bring mankind closer to salvation.

Members also point out that garments are better adapted to the African physique of Caribbean women than are European forms of dress. The long robes make women look majestic, they say, and the men appear strikingly royal. In addition, the robes give more freedom to both genders to dance and glorify the Lord, and to protect the women from appearing unseemly as they spin and writhe while under the influence of the Spirit. Consequently, there is no need to be constantly concerned about dresses riding up and showing off undergarments.

The personal significance of garments to individual members is not always easy to determine, and on occasion the information given me was revealed in the most unexpected of ways. On one occasion, I was casually chatting with a senior Church member about how she was feeling after a Sunday service. She proceeded to tell me that she was feeling very good and thankful for all that God had done for her. And then, as evidence of her blessings, she pointed to her garments and caressed them, as she explained that God had given them to her. He had looked out for her and made clear that she was important. She felt blessed and special. She then added an unexpected comment. She noted that no other church in Barbados had been able to provide her with spiritual garments. And as she continued to praise God and the Spiritual Baptist faith, I realized that she was not rushing to take off her garments and go home, even though the service was at an end. She wished to savour every extra moment of spiritual pleasure in wearing her garments.

On several other occasions, I unexpectedly came upon one member who was in the process of fixing the garments of another, making sure that the robes or stoles fell evenly or were draped as custom dictated. This pride in appearance or in the appearance of another member of the Church was striking. It translated a heightened respect for the garments themselves as well as for the process of wearing them.

Despite the appearance of satisfaction and contentment among many members with their garments and the process of garment allocation, it would be a mistake to conclude that all is well. For example, I had at first concluded that the system of wearing garments within the Spiritual Baptist faith essentially eliminated the class and economic distinctions of secular life. But members repeatedly reminded me that garments can be costly, and some members have to wait to have garments made until their resources improve. And even in olden days, some members complained that, in order to stay looking fresh and neat, the women had to have more than one white uniform, as they disliked wearing white garments that were stained or dirtied by the dust and dirt of tropical life. In addition, I thought at first that the wearing of garments served to democratize the structure in Spiritual Baptist churches, which is a desirable goal; however, there is still a vertical hierarchy extant in the Church, which we shall explore in the next chapter.

THE LEADER'S GARMENTS

We should pause here to consider the garments worn by Patriarch Granville Williams at the present time. My own observations have led me to conclude that he wears three different categories of garments, although one could legitimately argue that there is a fourth category stemming from his tendency to mix garments from the first three. The first category is characterized by a simple robe of the type worn at ceremonies in which he intends to do substantial work and wearing complicated robes would constitute a hindrance. Examples of such occasions are the Maundy Thursday service, when he anoints and washes the feet of members of his congregation, and the baptismal and mourning services, when rituals are complex and involve the purification, anointing, sealing and banding of members. On one of these occasions, for example, the Leader wore a head-tie formed by use of a red, blue and white striped towel, and a simple blue cotton robe tied at the waist by a red sash. Visible on the robe were seals or symbols melded into the fabric.

Figure 7.18 Archbishop Granville Williams addressing congregation at Maundy Thursday service, Jerusalem Cathedral. Barbados, 2008.

The second category of garment is usually more colourful and ornate. And although there is a simplicity about it that evokes the garments worn by the Spiritual Baptists of thirty years ago, there is, at the same time, a richness in the fabric that raises doubts that Leaders of long ago would have worn such attire. In the example here, the Leader's dress appears to be a yellow satin robe with crosses built into the material. He has a red sash or cincture around the waist and a small, bordeaux-coloured head-covering that recalls the kufi hat worn in Africa. The ensemble does not suggest a direct linkage to other mainstream religious movements in the Caribbean.

This apparel stands in direct contrast to the third category of garment worn by Williams, which indicates his position as an ordained member of a well-known, Christian, religious order. In the example here, the Archbishop wears a cream-coloured robe with a stole built into it. Detectable under the robe is a mauve clergy shirt indicating his rank, and on his head is a bishop's mitre. But these categories may be mixed, as I have said before. We see an example of this in his garments worn on the Good Friday pilgrimage described in chapter 5: at that time he wore white robe with a white chasuble, but on his head was the typical Spiritual Baptist towel.

One last point about Archbishop Williams's dress deserves emphasis, as it serves as a significant reminder: he may wear all of these different classes of robes, and still his feet may be bare. That is often the case when he is within the Church and the occasion or ritual is sacred. Obviously he wears shoes when he is on a Church pilgrimage in the community, as on Good Friday, but

Figure 7.19 Archbishop Granville Williams surrounded by followers at one Station of the Cross on Good Friday. Bridgetown, Barbados, 2008.

Figure 7.20 Archbishop Granville Williams leading retinue at a funeral service. Jerusalem Cathedral, Barbados, 2008.

Figure 7.21 Archbishop Granville Williams sitting next to the people's altar at Jerusalem Cathedral. Barbados, 2008.

he may also wear shoes within the Church at times when he will have to continue his functions outside, such as at a funeral, when he will have to proceed to a cemetery to inter the body. In the 1980s, when I first entered the Church, going without shoes inside the Church was a custom much more rigidly observed by all the members. In recent years, though, I have noticed that some women, for example, wear soft slippers resembling the footwear of ballet dancers. I have not seen members who were wearing shoes in the area of the high altar, however. Going without shoes is a reminder that the inside of the Church is holy ground.

As I have observed the changes in the Leader's garments over time, it appears evident that he has been influenced by the traditional styles of other Protestant and Catholic churches, even though he has retained distinctive characteristics of the Spiritual Baptist faith. So he wears the towel as a covering on his head, which I could find in no other faith group in Barbados. But I knew the stoles, surplices, and chasubles as a boy attending the Anglican Cathedral. Similarly, I had seen the rope cinctures worn around the waist well over fifty years ago. But I had never seen them worn in the style of lapcords. Finally, the Leader's own garments have seen the ultimate in their evolution, as he has been appointed a patriarch in the faith. The garments given to him on the day of his installation in that high office represented a move as far away as possible from the traditional simple robes of Spiritual Baptist Leaders from seventy-five years ago.

Leader Williams's garments therefore convey dynamism and historicity, even as there are language and symbolism in what he wears. The difficulty is in trying to understand what he means to say through his garments. And part of that difficulty is linked to the problem of grasping who his audience is at any particular time. But I have concluded, at the least, that garments are important to him, and that they add a distinctive dimension to the performative nature of his work as Leader of the Church. I grasped their importance as I came to appreciate the attention he has given over the years to the meticulous tailoring of garments for members of the congregation. Garments in themselves translate discipline to outsiders. They must not be constructed haphazardly. Their linkage to the Holy Spirit must be readily seen in the way they are worn, and a high level of spirituality must radiate from the garments and their wearers.

At the same time, these garments are Spiritual Baptist garments. So they

Figure 7.22 Archbishop Granville Williams at his ceremonial elevation to the Apostolic Patriarchate. Brooklyn, New York, 2008.

signify membership in a group that is unique and that has access to a special brand of Christianity. And while Williams appears to appropriate garments from other established religious groups for his use and that of his followers, the Spiritual Baptist imprint still remains on the final appearance and use of the garments. The Leader's garments therefore speak of his identity as a Spiritual Baptist Leader, but they also translate his sense of drama and aesthetics. Years ago, the garments may have been sedate and conservative. Now they symbolize beauty and radiance in a Caribbean sort of way, with the colours striking and vibrant. The Leader himself has been repeatedly described to me as "handsome" or "pretty" in the garments of Palm Sunday or Easter morning. Members have insisted to me that they have to look pretty and not let down their Leader as they prepare to go out in the community, where they will be observed by the public.

Yet, there is still ample room in what the Leader wears to see the heavy strand of spirituality, as well as the blend of authority and authenticity. The garments are not merely celebratory in appearance; they convey gravity and attention to the tasks of seeking salvation, of communicating with the prophets of the Old Testament, of remaining grounded in the history of black people in the Caribbean. In the last instance, in particular, appropriations from white-dominated religions are minimized and, as Leader, Williams is seeking space for black people in the Kingdom of God.

SUMMARY

Buturain's observations (2005) have reminded me of the significance of the visual images I have provided at the end of this chapter and elsewhere throughout this book. I have given my own descriptions and interpretations of the garments worn by members of the Spiritual Baptist faith group. But I recognize that I am neither an art historian nor a theologian, and I have tried feebly to come to terms with what other scholars, using a much more sharply honed lens, would have deduced from the images I have provided. Nevertheless, the pictures presented here certainly witness to the tradition of wearing garments in the Sons of God Apostolic Spiritual Baptist Church in Barbados.

These pictures will trigger varying associations in the minds of different people, as Buturain observes. Some will see evidence of community in the tableau of members of the congregation gathered around the Leader at a Station of the Cross on Good Friday. Most are dressed in white, and the contrast with their black faces suggests a potent reminder that citizens of the Third World also have access to the Saviour whose blood was shed to create redemption. The pictures of female members participating in a procession outside the

Church will translate a variety of messages: variety trumps uniformity in those images, and the sacred is transmitted here through a blaze of tropical colour that suggests elegance and beauty. But these same pictures remind me of connections to the past, to Africa and hints of India, and to lines of the female religious who have gone before. These particular pictures also create a sense of celebration and serenity, as they were taken on an Easter Sunday morning, when Churchgoers recall that Jesus is risen, and that the resurrection is a time of rejoicing.

One Church member repeatedly told me that the most important symbolic function of Spiritual Baptist garments resides in their inherent representation of an individual's spiritual rank and achievements. But this symbolic meaning may not in fact be evident to every observer. The uninitiated often miss this dimension of Spiritual Baptists' garments because they are easily seduced by the flashiness or the apparent elegance of the vestments. Yet, elegance and colour remain undisputedly sought-after characteristics of garments in the eyes of many members. People want to look good in what they wear, while at the same time conveying a deep sense of spirituality. This is easily seen in the survey of head-ties provided in this chapter. Several members confirmed that head-ties have evolved from simple white or red ones to head-ties of many different colours, tied around the head in different ways, sometimes resembling turbans and other times approximating what they call veils. Indeed, one woman stated plainly that some members have started adding brooches to their head-ties in a clear effort to look more attractive. So what is secular elegance or the work of the Holy Spirit is not easy to determine.

The same informant pointed out that the second most important function of a garment is its inherent capacity to produce a therapeutic effect on the wearer. In other words, the garment may make the wearer feel better and function more effectively in the secular world. The informant explained that wearing a garment for even an hour during a service may serve to extend the therapeutic effect over a period of days. Even so, some members wear a head-tie during their secular activities so as to carry certain feelings over into their workweek. Others wear their baptismal gowns to bed in an effort to make their sleep peaceful and blessed. Still others spend as many hours as possible in the garments they associate with a healing experience. Doing so seems to recapitulate, to repeat, the act of healing and to reinforce the psychological effect of the garments.

CHAPTER 8

Organizational Structure

I WOULD EXPECT STUDENTS of the Barbados Sons of God Apostolic Spiritual Baptist Church to have a pronounced interest in the organization of the Church for a number of reasons. First, understanding the structure should provide some insight into the thinking of the Church's founder about how he fits his role into the ecclesiastical conceptualization of the organization. Organizational structure also translates how secular ideas such as democracy, fairness and rewards fit into the spiritual vision of the Church. Finally, the structural organization of any entity always gives some information about its long-term viability. For example, who is empowered to make decisions and who controls the finances of the organization may speak volumes about the attention being paid to the organization's future. The faith has survived in the face of considerable persecution over the years, which has raised the question about what structural factors have contributed to the faith's longevity. Of equal interest is the tendency of Spiritual Baptist churches to stay small, which makes observers wonder about the structural impediments to growth and expansion.

The first organizational element to consider in the Barbados Church is the internal ranks used to carry out the Church's rituals and to accomplish tasks set by the Leader in furtherance of the primary mission of spreading the Gospel and caring for members of the congregation. As I have suggested before, especially in talking about mourning and discussing the connection between ranks and garments, ranks carry prestige and honour. Furthermore, the rank system establishes a hierarchy within any Spiritual Baptist church.

Consequently, ranks promote members' ideas about advancement within the organization and catalyse ambition, even as everyone repeats time and again that one's rank is the measure solely of one's spiritual depth.

Spiritual Baptists have long advocated and supported this dimension of each church's internal structure, and have linked ranks to the concept of democratizing the organization. But ranks also formally emphasize the Spiritual Baptist notion that not everyone in a church is at the same point of spiritual development at any given time. In addition, the work within the Church, what transpires as the collective is publicly worshipping God, has multiple and different functions that cannot be carried out by the same people all the time. This is so because each member has received different gifts from the Holy Spirit. Some preach, others heal and still others may be teachers and explicate the gospel to the inexperienced in Christ. There is, however, another important reason for not limiting Church functions to any one constituency within the group: spreading out Church work results in the involvement of the largest number of people. This in turn is thought to lead to the enhancement of the entire congregation's sense of participation and ownership of all that transpires within the organization. This Spiritual Baptist theory has been seen as a legitimate response to the early days of slavery and colonial life when blacks were kept from full participation in church services.

INTERNAL RANKS OF OTHER SPIRITUAL BAPTIST CHURCHES

I think it is useful, before proceeding, to consider the ranks used in the Barbados Church, as well as to review the ranks described by observers of other Spiritual Baptist churches outside of Barbados. This survey should establish a reference point for comparison and allow readers to reflect more easily on the meaning and significance of ranks within the traditional structure of a Spiritual Baptist church. Nevertheless, I must emphasize that rigid comparisons could be misleading. Readers must understand that no two Spiritual Baptist churches are exactly alike, and that the tradition of individual church autonomy has been around a very long time. In addition, comparing a church on one island to a church on another is only useful if the observer can flexibly reflect on the similarities and differences without trying to reach value judgements.

Glazier (1983) has described in some detail the internal ranks of the churches he studied in Trinidad. He states that the Spiritual Baptists on that island recognize ranks that are associated with specific duties, and he notes that these ranks are revealed through the mourning ceremony. He names the following ranks: Provers, Preachers, Shepherds, Captains, Pointers, Bell Ringers, Water Carriers, Water Fetchers, Postmen, Healers, Divers, Watchmen, Surveyors, Nurses, Teachers, Leaders, Mothers, Sisters, Brothers, Warriors, Commanders, Inspectors and Judges.

Glazier states that the highest ranks, in descending order, are Judges, Inspectors, Commanders and Warriors. Then come the Teachers and Pointers, who are on the same level; they are followed by the Captains, Provers and Divers, who are all of equal rank. On the next level are the Mothers and Leaders. After them come the Surveyors, Shepherds, Postmen, Watchmen, Nurses and Preachers, all grouped on the same level. Finally, placed on the bottom two levels are the Water Fetchers and Water Carriers (who are grouped together), with the least prestigious ranks being the Sisters and Brothers. Glazier notes that, in this organizational structure, a member could well move horizontally in title before moving vertically, a state of affairs that apparently provokes some complaining from members who are tired of long waits before they can experience significant promotions within their churches. Glazier also emphasizes that the connection between mourning visions and the subsequent acquisition of Church rank is not as direct as was previously emphasized by other researchers. He postulates that the significant element connecting visions with promotion within the ranks is the final interpretation given to the visions by the Leaders of the churches. As a result, experienced mourners are in some cases suspected of describing the types of visions they know will have the greatest impact on their Leaders.

Without performing a detailed comparative analysis of Glazier's ranks, I must still make several clear statements about his findings. First, the ranks of Judges, Inspectors, Commanders and Warriors do not exist within the Barbados Church. These ranks, in Trinidad, are said to be ultimately responsible for settling disputes between high-ranking Church members, and also serve as the court of last resort on matters of Church policy. In the Barbados Church, however, these functions are clearly the responsibility of the Leader. Similarly, the functions of proving and pointing exist in the Barbados Church, but are carried out by members who do not carry the specific titles of Prover or

Pointer. This is likewise the case for the functions of surveying, which I have described in chapter 5. While the act of surveying exists in the Barbados Church, no one carries the title of Surveyor.

In the Trinidadian Church, the Preachers are authorities in the interpretation of scripture and, I presume, explicate scriptural texts during the part of the worship service when they preach their sermons. Again, in the Barbados Church, this function is taken very seriously but it is not assigned to anyone called a Preacher. Indeed, a look at the type of activity carried out by Trinidadian "Preachers" leads to discussion of the development of what is called the Ministerial Order in the Barbados Church. But preaching and interpretation of the Bible are functions of the entire Church in Barbados, and the ultimate arbiter of all debates in this area is without doubt the Leader.

The rank of Postman is, of course, nonexistent in the Barbados Church of today. With the ubiquitous presence of telephones on the island, no one is needed to carry a message to distant country sites as may have been necessary forty or fifty years ago. I am in frequent contact with several Church members from overseas by telephone as well as through the internet, which speaks volumes about the participation of Barbados and the Church in the new revolution of information technology. While it is obvious that the ageing Leader of the Barbados Church is not a vibrant user of this new technology, he makes constant use of Church members who are at ease with it.

Perhaps the most stable roles in the Barbados Church, ones that are currently readily recognized, are the Nurses and Mothers. Indeed, among the oldest female members are some individuals who are still respectfully called by their former titles of Mother, even though they had moved on to a higher rank. Recently I was seeking to find the house of a member who had agreed to be interviewed by me. I found her neighbourhood but could not identify her house. Neighbours in the community came to my aid once I made clear that I was looking for Mother James (not her real name), the honorific title that she had acquired many years ago. Mothers also have broader duties than those linked to mourning, as is the case in the Trinidadian churches described by Glazier. A Mother has garnered wide-ranging respect within the Church by dint of her experience, her deep spirituality and the way she carries herself. Yes, she serves in the mourning room like the Nurses, and she is also very visibly present at baptismal ceremonies like the Nurses. But the Mother in Barbados is not a Nurse, as is evident by the difference in their garments. Even so, garments are not really what distinguishes them, except to outsiders. Their carriages are substantially different: the Mother is definite and confident in all that she does, and even as she is obedient to the Leader, there is no element of obsequiousness in the way she carries out his instructions.

In Henney's observations (1982) of the Vincentian churches that she conducted in the 1960s, she describes the following ranks: the Pointer is the highest position in the Church and is followed by the Leader, who is considered an apprentice to the Pointer or a Pointer-in-training. Henney notes that Pointers and Leaders are men, and states that the symbols of a Pointer's status, given to him in his spiritual travels, are a belt, basin, towel, bell, Bible and gown. In comparison to the attributes assigned in the Barbados Church, these tools are quite interesting. The belt, towel and gown no longer have the same significance, because garments worn in Barbados have evolved well beyond this simplicity. I have also never heard in Barbados that the basin is such an important element, although it certainly has a significant role to play in the purification rituals I have already described in the section on baptism (see chapter 5). In Barbados, the bell, Bible and lota are noted to be the defining elements of the Spiritual Baptists.

Henney also mentions other positions in the Vincentian churches, such as that of Captain, a rank that she says is, in a sense, comparable to that of the head of a ship – someone who can lead the whole crew in the Spirit. She also identifies the position of Preacher, even as she explains that some men have served in this quite high position without having gone to mourn. Such an observation, of course, is tantamount to raising once again the question about how some members have to rely on mourning to secure advancement, while others depend more clearly on their relationships to the individuals in the Church who have the authority to make appointments to different ranks.

Henney also names the position of Mother, adding that there are different degrees within that rank for women. Hence, there are Mother Matrons, Mother Helpers, Assistance Mothers and Queen Mothers. But, in general, the rank of Mother symbolizes a prestigious position for women who seem capable of performing almost any task in the Church. Often, their activities are duplicated by Nurses. Henney also mentions the rank of Warrior, someone delegated to sit close to the centre-pole and participate in the process of adoption, which is defined as the making of sweet musical sounds while under the influence of the Holy Spirit. Warriors do not exist in the Barbados scheme.

The observations of Henney and of Glazier are significant, as they provide some reference point for us to use as we consider the ranks found in Barbados. It should be remembered, however, that Henney's findings are now about forty years old. And although Glazier's work is more recent, there has been considerable economic and socio-educational change throughout the Caribbean since the time of those earlier anthropological research expeditions. In a sense, the Barbados of today may be years away from what was being done in St Vincent and Trinidad of yesteryear. For example, Henney states that members who have obtained certain ranks through mourning are entitled to wear the insignia of those ranks; a Warrior, for instance, can wear the rosette of that office on her dress. In discussing the wearing of insignia, Henney describes one Mother O, who was entitled to wear a rope around her waist and a special dress, as well as an apron and a bib. But Mother O usually wore only the rope around the waist of an ordinary dress. This cavalier approach to wearing the insignia of rank is clearly not the custom in the present-day Barbados Church.

INTERNAL RANKS OF THE BARBADOS CHURCH

The Barbados Church described its own internal ranks in a programme booklet issued to celebrate the thirtieth anniversary of the Church's founding. The booklet was titled "The Revelations of Spiritual Baptists in Barbados" and was produced in December 1987. I have utilized the list of ranks as presented in that programme and have combined it with information obtained in my own interviews with members of the Church to produce the list of ranks delineated in table 1. The ranks listed in the 1987 programme are not up to date, which justified my efforts to obtain additional information. For example, the 1987 listing does not include the rank of Abbess, which is currently occupied by about six women. Indeed, that rank is now subdivided into several degrees. The 1987 listing also included Sub-Deacons, but several current members stated that they could not recall the last time that someone was named to that rank. Of course, since 1987, two Bishops have been consecrated by Archbishop Williams in the Barbados Church. Table 1 represents the consensus of a number of members' understanding of and views on the ranks within the Church. The table was not created from information provided unilaterally by the Leader, as I wished to grasp the views of members, who indeed made clear to

Table 8.1 Ranks in the Barbados Spiritual Baptist Church

ORDER	AGE GROUP	FEMALES	MALES
Non-Ministerial	*Children*	Rosebuds	Sacred Hearts
	Young Adolescents	Damsels	Sacred Hearts
	Older Adolescents	Daughters of Salem	Prince Shepherds
	Adults	League of Mary Ambassadors Nurses Teachers Teacher Captains Superior Captains Grand Superior Captains	Knights of Jerusalem Good Samaritans Captains Superior Captains
Ministerial	*Adults*	Deaconesses Mothers of the Church (#1, #2) Reverend Mothers Mothers of Sorrow Elders Abbesses Queen Abbesses Queen Grand Abbesses	Deacons Reverends High Priests Arch-High Priests Elders Bishops Archbishop Patriarch

me that there is considerable overlap and elasticity in the ranks and their functions. Actual examples provided by members will make that clear. The members themselves made the sharp distinctions between the roles of women and men.

I would like to review table 1 in some detail. Neither of the scholars mentioned earlier specifically focuses attention on ranks for children and adolescents. In the Barbados Church, these positions exist, which is, in itself, significant, because it makes clear that children do have some role in the Church, although that role is relatively measured. The participation of children responds to societal need, however, as Barbadian mothers, especially, still like to take their young children to church, believing that it is important to start their children off in church at an early age in order to provide them a solid Christian grounding. As parents say frequently in Barbados, what their children do later on after they have matured is up to them, but they cannot say that they have never seen the inside of a church. In addition, even in the present day, many mothers have no one to supervise their children while they go to church. As a result, the most convenient option is to take the children to church with them.

There is some fluidity of movement between the ranks of children and adolescents. No sharp age distinction exists, and progression from one group to another no doubt depends on the size and maturity of the individual. Some, for example, skip ranks in their promotions. Also, as other scholars have noted, promotions do not depend solely on the visions experienced during mourning. There is no doubt that, in the Barbados Church, the Leader has the prerogative to determine when people advance, independent of whether or not the individuals have mourned.

When I was organizing the material I had collected on ranks in the Barbados Church, I considered delineating clearly the specific duties for each rank. But, in the process of doing so, I accumulated so many exceptions that the method became problematic. Still, there are certain important functions worth clarifying and understanding so that observers may appreciate who carries the main responsibility for these activities. Put another way, certain ranks stand out as carrying the major responsibilities for specific duties. The Nurses, for example, are readily granted the charge of looking after candidates for baptism and making sure those candidates are observing the correct rituals and stances as the service proceeds. Nurses are also expected to care for members who become ill during a service.

The Knights of Jerusalem and the Ambassadors carry out the largely symbolic function of guarding the entrances to the Church. But the Knights are also expected to take seriously the function of security. These days this activity seems less important. But I recall well an episode about twenty-five years ago at the smaller Church in Richmond when a group of passers-by threw stones at the Church. This occurred at a time when the Church and its members were often persecuted because of their membership in the group. Several young male members of the Church responded so quickly and vigorously to the attack that I knew that the perpetrators must have run off promptly. The Church group was willing to defend their faith and the members' youthful athleticism and numbers would certainly have intimidated the perpetrators.

The Mothers of Sorrow have the charge of officiating in the mourning room. But if the number of mourners is large, then other groups are expected to assist the Mothers. The Mothers have now been expanded, as shown in table 1, to include Mothers #1 and #2, the latter rank being senior to the former. The Reverend Mothers, or Mother Reverends as I have also heard them called, is the rank naturally following that of Deaconesses. The rank utilizing the term Priests is solely allocated to men, but women may be Elders.

In the average Church service, there are routine functions to be carried out, such as surveying the building with the lota and bell, praying, reading lessons, delivering homilies or small sermons, taking up collection, protecting members who are in the Spirit from self-harm, and preparing the implements used in the service of Holy Communion. I have seen members of all the adult ranks above Ambassadors and Knights of Jerusalem participate in these activities. The very senior ranks of the Ministerial Order, however, tend to let others step forward first. It is uncommon to see an Elder or an Abbess performing a task such as surveying the Church.

Here a few words should be said about the Ministerial Order, which comprises certain groups, as noted in table 1. These ranks are seated at the front of the Church, and they may often be identified by their wearing the type of collar that is worn by ministers in many other denominations. They are expected to safeguard the Christian integrity of the Church, to preach and to help with the services of Holy Communion and the traditional rituals of christening, baptism, marriage and burial. It should be noted that women may now rise to impressive heights in the Barbados Church and, as Abbesses, they occupy ranks that are said to be the equivalent of Bishop and Archbishop. In other words, women enjoy substantial prestige in the group. They may not, however, ascend to the position of Leader of the Church.

One custom that seems to have taken hold in the Church is the dividing of some ranks into degrees, which permits some members to gain an acknowledged seniority without moving out of their ranks *per se*. For example, within the rank of Teacher Captain, one may now be promoted to Superior Captain and Grand Superior Captain. This type of promotion often permits a member to keep the same basic uniform of the Teacher Captain, for example, while only having to change the aspects of the garment that are less expensive. In the group of Mothers, as I have already noted, there is now Group #1 and Group #2, indicating a differentiation in status. Among the Abbesses, the Queen Abbesses and Queen Grand Abbesses outrank Abbesses.

Relatively recently, Elson (2007) has provided a list of the ranks in the Barbados Church. But my informants have suggested corrections to his list, although they emphasize that the ranks have changed over time. So, for example, Elson lists Preachers, Temple Guards, Divers and Leaders as ranks for men. I have verified that these ranks no longer exist, although their functions have not been eliminated. Similarly, there are no longer Divers among the women.

Despite the elaboration of ranks and the assignment of them to cover all the activities within the Church, new tasks have been established that are covered by specific individuals. These tasks could be considered administrative posts that do not fundamentally change a member's basic rank, although they add to an individual's standing within the group. Examples of these posts include Dean of the Cathedral, Archdeacon, Censer and Vicar General. Only one person holds each post. The Dean makes sure that the Cathedral service runs smoothly and that the service functions are carried out effectively and in an orderly fashion. The Censer is an Elder charged with the management of incense during the service at the Cathedral. Even observation of many services, however, still never clarified specifically the responsibilities of the Archdeacon and Vicar General. It is possible that their administrative duties are actually executed outside of Church services and behind the scenes.

Another group of functions emerged during my many observations of the Church's activities. This class of work could not be said to be properly within traditional ecclesiastical functions. Nevertheless, these roles are without a doubt essential to the smooth functioning of the group's labours. For example, there is one member of the Ministerial Order who is in charge of the complicated sound system in the Cathedral. This individual does more than just look after the microphones used during the service. He helps to prepare the tapes used by a local radio station that broadcasts a Spiritual Baptist service on a weekly basis. He also puts together the hymns and sacred music that can be heard in the Cathedral before and after the usual Sunday services, as well as before and after special events, such as funerals and weddings.

Another example of these special roles is the group of individuals who run the canteen where food and drinks can be bought on Sundays. As previously discussed, Sunday services can run for many hours. Church members like to boast that the duration of a service depends on the movement of the Spirit, and they delight in saying that if one leaves home to go praise God, then why should one be rushing to go elsewhere? Of course, the pressure to leave the services is alleviated by the convenience of being able to purchase food and drink. And the food is not merely snacks. Full meals are available – chicken and rice, macaroni and cheese, flying fish, and so on – followed by the usual dessert of Barbadian pound cake or something similar. As in the case of the extensive sound system, the existence of the canteen is testimony to the large size of the congregation as well as to the imposing nature of the edifice.

One unusual group that I encountered during my observations of the Church was called the Archbishop's Court. This group is made up of both men and women who attend the Leader during services. They are specially selected by him and are without doubt a prestigious body. Some of them are always within a few steps of the Leader whenever he is carrying out his functions, ready to transmit a message from him to another member of the Church or to support the Leader's execution of a particular ritual. Members of the Archbishop's Court may on some occasions (for example, on the Leader's trips overseas) wear a distinctive garment that differentiates them from others. In my interviews of members over the years, many have spoken of this group in almost sacred tones. Constant proximity to the Leader is a special reward for members of the Archbishop's Court, and I naturally assumed that some members long to be chosen for the group. Only one member, however, talked to me straightforwardly about desiring this assignment. In recent months I have learned that the Leader announced some time ago that he was looking to expand the group. He invited members to express their interest in joining his court, but I never learned how many members stepped forward to state their wishes. The member who spoke of having an interest in joining the group could not explain why there was shyness about acknowledging such a desire. I concluded that members must find something unacceptable about squarely confronting an inner urge to be a member of the court, perhaps because something about it seems brash and peculiarly non-spiritual, as though members who desire that kind of status seem to be showing off rather than waiting quietly for the Holy Spirit to manifest the answer to the question of whether a particular individual deserves the honour.

The following examples describe different routes that individuals took in moving through the ranks of the Barbados Spiritual Baptist Church.

EXAMPLE 1

This particular man entered the Church after baptism as an adult and was a member of the Knights of Jerusalem for about two years. A committee of the Knights then recommended his advancement to the Good Samaritans, and he served in that group for several years. He recalled clearly that, as a Knight, he guarded the Temple with a wooden sword or with a shepherd's rod, but he could not provide the same specificity for what he did as a Good Samaritan. His next promotion was to the Ministerial Order, where he began as a Sub-Deacon, learning how to participate in the rituals of the worship services. After about four years, he was ordained a Deacon, and he remained in that rank for a few years, continuing his training as a minister of the Church, before he was ordained as a Reverend. In this example, the member bypassed the ranks of Captain and Superior Captain. It is not clear what factors influenced this particular route of advancement. Also, moving to the rank of Sub-Deacon cannot be said to be a promotion above Captain and Superior Captain, at least not in every case. I have witnessed several Captains participating prominently and visibly in Church services. When I asked questions about the roles of those who occupy these positions, it was made clear to me that they are considered to be deeply spiritual and carry out advanced functions in Church services because of their recognized abilities.

EXAMPLE 2

This middle-aged female joined the Church and, after being baptized, was assigned to the League of Mary, in which she remained for about five years. As a member of a group of spiritual beginners, her duties were minimal, and she was only occasionally invited to read a lesson during a Church service. Her next assignment was to the Teachers' Association, where she carried out functions of reading lessons and preparing the altars for Church services. She remained a teacher for over a decade and eventually won a promotion to teacher captain. In that rank she participated in the mourning services and in the preparation of candidates for baptism. After almost two decades spent at that level, she was named to the Ministerial Order at the rank of Mother Reverend, bypassing the status of Deaconess. She pointed out that her most recent promotion was not obtained through the mourning process. Rather, she felt confident that her long and committed service to the Church had been recognized by the Leader, and that he had discerned her growth in the Spirit over the years.

EXAMPLE 3

In this example, the young woman explained that she started out her life in the Church as a member of the Rosebuds, which she joined as a little girl. On special occasions the Rosebuds appeared in the aisles of the Church; at other times they attended Sunday school classes. From time to time, the Rosebuds read scripture passages during a Church service. Around age twelve, she joined the group of Damsels, who carried out essentially the same functions as the older Rosebuds. As she became an older adolescent, she was promoted to the Daughters of Salem group, in which she read lessons and also held candles while others were reading the lessons. Eventually, she stopped attending Church, drawn away by other secular interests. She returned to Church some years later while she was still a young adult. At first she sat at the back of the Church and concentrated on the task of maturing spiritually, without participating directly in the services. After continuing in this way for about seven years, the Leader sent for her one Sunday during a service. Other members escorted her to the altar, where she was anointed by the Leader and given the lapcords of a teacher captain. With this investiture, she had skipped over a number of other ranks, as can be seen by looking at table 1. In addition, she was completely surprised by the Leader's action and had had no premonition through a vision that she would be blessed in this way.

OTHER ADMINISTRATIVE STRUCTURES

In the description of the Church's administration that was published in the programme of the thirtieth anniversary service (1987), mention is made of the Supreme Council and the Grand Council. These Councils are described in the programme as the "highest decision making entities" and are said to be the bodies that formulate Church doctrine and directives. Members told me unambiguously, however, that both groups were no longer functioning in 2009, and that they had not functioned for a long time. Apparently, when these groups were functioning, the Grand Council was made up of senior members of the Church, of whom the Leader was chairman. The members of the Supreme Council were drawn from among ministers who sat on the Grand Council. The inactive status of these two bodies led me inexorably to the conclusion that important decisions about the Church can now only be made in two ways.

First, a subject can be discussed at what is called the Church's General Meeting. This usually takes place at the Cathedral in Ealing Grove on a weekday evening. I attended several of these meetings in 2009. At those meetings the attendance was low and varied between fifteen and thirty people. The Leader chaired the proceedings, and anyone could bring up a topic for discussion. In one meeting that I attended in March 2009, the Leader spoke with members in a conversational way about the meaning of Lent and described the continuing struggle between the Church and the world, urging members to stand up for Jesus. He went on to mention the difficulties in building and maintaining a church. For example, he pointed out that a thriving church should have attached to it organizations such as a day-care centre, a hospital and a school. He said he had not received enough support to be that successful in what he had built. But he had always had, as a central mission, the idea of transforming the Eurocentric orientation of Barbadian Christian society into a more Afrocentric position. After he spoke about these ideas, he opened up the floor to comments from others.

One member stood and praised the Leader as "real" and called him a man sent by God. This member noted that, in the recent history of the Church, jealousy had been motivating some members to attack the Leader. But, the speaker argued, members should instead be grateful for the Archbishop's leadership. The speaker went on to emphasize that their organization was a church, not a political party, and excoriated the few members who were trying to divide the Church. The Archbishop later took up this thread in his reply. He mentioned his disappointment at the controversy and emphasized that, for the Church to go on, everyone must be on the same road that he is on. He added that he has already shown everyone the road he is taking, which is the path to God.

In another General Meeting I attended, a young man stood and presented the idea of starting a scout troop for young people. The Leader replied that it was a good idea and continued to discuss it, but I was surprised by the way in which the discussion ended. No one spoke against the suggestion, and the Leader never gave a clear endorsement to the recommendation. The conclusion seemed particularly nebulous to me. After the meeting, I spoke to the young man and learned that he had served as the assistant leader of a troop elsewhere and was ready to put his energy to developing a movement in his own home Church. He also introduced me to another young man with similar scouting experience who was ready to help. I then wished him good luck, hoping that he would find a way to overcome the tepid support he had received. But this example, and the previous one, at least showed how the General Meeting could be used.

I also encountered several examples of another usage for the General Meeting – as a form of ecclesiastical court. (I have alluded to this function before in earlier chapters.) Several members informed me of one of the most recent trials, which took place at a General Meeting in 2009. I learned that the Archbishop had asked the Secretary of the Church to summon a member to attend this meeting. The member was given no further information in the formal summons about what was to transpire, although he did learn some details from others, as there is clearly an informal communications system at work in the Church. But it was not until the meeting itself, apparently, that the member learned from the Leader exactly what charges he was facing.

Members who provided me information about this meeting were in agreement that the accused member was not allowed to speak on his own behalf, although some other Church members did provide witness in his support. One particular point of contention had to do with the fact that the Archbishop had refused to identify the members who had provided information to him about what the accused member had allegedly done. The meeting apparently concluded with a punishment being meted out by the Leader. Obviously, there was no route of appeal, as the Archbishop had spoken. And some members of the Church were aggrieved by the process, which, in their opinion, had been short-circuited and essentially dominated by the Leader, at least with respect to the punishment. I did not proceed to try to verify the truthfulness or accuracy of the accusations flying back and forth. That was not my role. But I was interested in clarifying how the General Meeting structure could be used.

I learned later in 2009 that another incident had occurred, in which one member reportedly used threatening language to another. The matter was apparently reported to the Leader. (Once again, my interest here is not the veracity or precision of the accusation, but only the procedure used to reach a resolution to the problem.) Members told me that the Leader had spoken to both members involved, presumably to find out what had actually occurred. He then brought up the incident in a Sunday morning service, during which he interrupted the ritual and announced the punishment of the presumably guilty party. It was a two-week period of exclusion from the Church. At the end of that period, again in a Sunday morning service, both of the involved members were called to the front of the Church and asked to greet each other in fellowship, using the classic Spiritual Baptist ritualistic interaction that starts with the locking of hands. The arms are then extended laterally as the individuals draw closer and touch chest to chest and right cheek to right cheek. After ritualistically embracing each other, they step back and withdraw their hands. This ceremonial greeting of fellowship symbolizes the dissolution of strife in the context of forgiving and forgetting and reminds individuals that they are one body in Christ. Members who are not at odds with each other often use this greeting to celebrate their unity. In this particular instance, the Leader told the two women to return to their seats and be at peace.

It appeared that, with the Archbishop's intervention, the two members had reconciled their differences, although no one may ever be really sure of it. I was surprised to learn that the Leader had handled this matter outside of the General Meeting structure, but the episode does show the power of the Leader to circumvent established structures at will. Of course, it is easy to imagine situations when such potential informality serves the interest of the organization. For example, in this case, the party responsible for the grievance – assuming that the accused was in fact guilty and had taken responsibility for what had transpired – avoided a more public airing of the entire case at a General Meeting. At the same time, however, resorting to informality and avoiding confrontation with the complainant and witnesses may have abridged the rights of the accused, who may have lost esteem and standing in the eyes of other group members. It is not clear either that the offended party in a case such as this was pleased with the informality of the proceedings. Perhaps this plaintiff wanted to milk the complaint for all it was worth. If that were the case, the Leader certainly could be applauded for representing the broader interests of the organization and its members and protecting the Church from further scandal, while still confronting the conflict.

A COMPARATIVE VIEW

I discussed the business of structure with other ministers in Barbados and settled on a Pentecostal group that had some elements in common with Spiritual Baptist philosophy. Again, there was no intent to establish a comparative system that would result in judgements one way or the other about the Spiritual Baptist structure. But I was seeking a way to conceptualize what Archbishop Williams has established so that I might understand better what the group may consider as they look to the future and determine what changes they may wish to assess, whether or not they are actually implemented.

Certain structural elements stand out in the Pentecostal Church's scheme. There are about twelve churches operating on the island, with a pastor assigned to each church. One of these pastors also serves as the presiding Bishop, who in turn has responsibility to the leadership of the church headquarters, located in the United States. Under the local Bishop in Barbados is a committee of Elders drawn from among the group of pastors. Below the pastor in each church is an organizational structure that copies the structure I have seen in many churches, regardless of denomination: assistant ministers, deacons, ushers, men's fellowship group and so on. Included in this structure is the formal position of Treasurer, with responsibility for handling funds and giving an annual report to the congregation as well as to the presiding Bishop and the Elders. Any member of a church may take a complaint to the local pastor or may bypass the pastor and go to the Elders or presiding Bishop.

The Pentecostal structure offers the opportunity to reflect on what the Barbados Spiritual Baptists have in place under the leadership of their Archbishop. First, the Pentecostals have an appeals structure in place that affords the option of seeking advice from a pastor or bypassing him to go directly to the Elders or to the presiding Bishop. As a last resort, one may even take business to the leadership in North America. This promptly raises the question of whether a member of the Barbados Spiritual Baptists may complain to or seek advice from the Patriarchate located in New York City. Second, the handling of money seems to be a secretive matter for the Spiritual Baptists, while the Pentecostal group at least theoretically has a method for annual discussion of its finances. Many members of Williams's church have, however, informed me that the Archbishop has invested his own money in the Church, and that the Church is constructed on his own land. As any businessperson will witness, there are advantages to having informal structures that permit flexibility in the handling of funds. But the potential pitfalls of such mechanisms are also widely known. Indeed, it should also be noted that more formalized structures also permit shenanigans, as even members of these types of structures can be duped into making bad decisions.

The comparison between the Pentecostal and Spiritual Baptist groups forces us to return to consideration of a central question, one that has been brought up on several occasions by people outside the Church with whom I have held repeated conversations. The question centres on the problem of determining what is the most effective and useful mixture of modern administrative techniques and powerful spiritual values. Colleagues have reminded me that this question is repeatedly discussed, for example, at every monastery in the world, especially those with weak financial resources. And the debate goes on in colleges and universities all over the globe. As fiscal resources shrink, fights erupt over whether fiscal administrators or those imbued with the spirit of the educational mission, whatever that may be, should run the academy. Future generations will no doubt still be arguing about whether the Leader's style of management is best for the Spiritual Baptist Church.

GENDER ROLES AND ORGANIZATIONAL STRUCTURE

In regard to gender roles in the Church, Barbados Spiritual Baptists like to point to 1 Corinthians 3: "But I would have you know that the head of every man is Christ: and the head of the woman is the man: and the head of Christ is God." They use this verse to justify certain beliefs that the Church espouses as Spiritual Baptist orthodoxy, particularly the idea that women were never given charge over men. In addition, they claim that women are not allowed to officiate at the high altar during worship. More importantly, the restrictions on women have been extended to argue that no woman can be the head of a Spiritual Baptist church. Of course, this latter point is hotly disputed by other Spiritual Baptist groups, some of which have flatly rejected this notion, and women are known to lead churches on other islands. What is also ironic is that there is a Vincentian Spiritual Baptist church located not far from the Cathedral in Ealing Grove, Christ Church, and that small church is directed by a woman.

I do not mean to suggest that the Barbados Spiritual Baptists claim that women occupy a lesser spiritual status than men. I cannot make that case. In addition, even superficial observation of the Church leads to the obvious conclusion that women are important members of the Church. They make significant contributions to the worship services and play major roles in practically every event in which the Church participates. I have also been told that the senior Abbesses of the Church carry equivalent prestige to that of a Bishop or Archbishop. But still, they may not lead the Barbados Church.

I have found different responses to this state of affairs among the female members of the Church whom I interviewed. One senior female in the Church stated clearly that she believed a woman should not lead the group. At the same time, however, she made clear that no Church is complete without a woman, and she advocated the position that women and men should work together. In her view, each is the helpmate of the other. At first I wondered whether this view represented in general the philosophy of older women in the Church. But I found other younger females who essentially agreed with this position. I was also made to understand that young males in the Church agreed with this view. And I must add that I encountered young, university-educated males and females who had all embraced this line of argument.

In Rowe's examination (1985) of this subject among the Rastafari of Jamaica, she notes that Rastafari doctrine articulates clear views on females. For example, women can only be called to Rastafari through men and cannot lead any Rastafari ritual. Likewise, women cannot experience the highest heights of Rastafari without a man; males are the physical and spiritual head of the female and the family; and females are unclean whenever they have an issue of blood. Rowe points out that Rastafari doctrine is based on the Bible – and that the Bible therefore played a large part in determining the attitude of males to females in Rastafari – and confirms the basic point that Rastafari was a patriarchal movement. Rowe goes on to document, however, that ideas about the place of women in Rastafari were undergoing transformation as early as the late 1970s and 1980s. No doubt this was a function of all the civil rights changes influencing relationships between men and women in general, and black men and women in particular. These changes were expected to have an impact on the equality of access of both men and women to educational and economic opportunities. But the expected changes were also awaited in the arena of personal and group identity. Rowe anticipated that the place of women in the Rastafari movement would ultimately undergo transformation with the passage of time.

Hence, I was surprised in 2009 by some of my findings about the roles of women among the Barbados Spiritual Baptists. Women themselves seemed to accept that they held a position subsidiary to that of men. I noted, for example, that several women accepted the idea that only a man could lead the Church and carry out activities on the high altar. But they also agreed with the notion that a woman who was having her menstrual period should be considered unclean and unable therefore to participate in certain rituals such as mourning. I emphasize that some of the women holding this position were university-educated.

Not surprisingly, however, the whole story is not as simple and straightforward as that. This was brought home to me quite forcefully when I attended the consecration and elevation of the Archbishop to the Patriarchate. I approached one woman and asked her what she thought of the proceedings. Without losing a beat or taking time to contemplate her response, she asked me to sit down so that I could listen to her attentively without having bystanders able to eavesdrop on our conversation. Then, with minimal interruption from me, she made clear what a sacred shame it was that the authorities in charge could only find men to elevate to the status of patriarchs. And she lambasted the men for such provincial thinking, while striking a feminist pose that she believed was the true reflection of equality of all human beings in the sight of God. She attributed her understanding of this truth as a solid reason for her robust identity as a black woman.

Young men I interviewed in the Barbados Church would, I imagine, easily respond to this point that women in that Church have access to mourning. Women are promoted to senior ranks and they have unhindered access to the ministerial ranks of the Church, unlike what transpires in many other traditional denominations. And so, the debate will go on. Elson (2007) has provided an elegant analysis of the gender struggle in the Barbados Spiritual Baptist Church, noting that it is a powerful symbol of gender interaction in postcolonial Barbados. Still, gender interaction is complicated. And despite the obvious efforts of the men to hold on to their status and claim organizational superiority over women in faith groups, substantial changes are rapidly unfolding in secular society. For example, there have been female judges, female university professors and even a female Governor General of the island.

It will be important for scholars to follow this dimension of the Barbados Spiritual Baptist Church's orthodoxy as time passes. But I believe that Elson (2007) has it right in emphasizing that the older matriarchy in the group may be quietly supporting the males' efforts to contain the ambitions of the younger, university-educated women. This undermining of other females' dreams and aspirations for positions in Church hierarchy may be a throwback to the African matriarchal structure of yesteryear. But the women's psychological health and their self-identity are now solidly linked to equality of access and opportunity, and I have my doubts that the impediments to progress will withstand the women's demands.

Nevertheless, it is clear that women in these Caribbean religious contexts continue to be treated with some ambivalence or occupy positions that carry ambivalent status. Duncan (2001) thoughtfully explores the Aunt Jemima symbol among Spiritual Baptists in Toronto, Canada, and notes that the symbol seems to carry simultaneous contradictory traits of spiritual mother and servile woman. And Lake (1994) noted earlier this same paradox among Rastafarian women in Jamaica, who oscillate between poles of liberation and subordination. In my view, this paradox of contradiction and ambivalence captures well the situation of women in the Barbados Spiritual Baptist Church. Women are undoubtedly important in the organization and they enjoy relatively unfettered freedom to carry out their functions as they lead the Church in prayer, read lessons, preach, survey the Church and contribute to a host of other activities. But still, they must be subordinate to a male Leader, a requirement that must throw some water on the flames of parity and aspiration.

CHAPTER 9

Further Reflections on the Leader

AT A DINNER WITH friends in 2008, the conversation turned to the research that I had been doing in Barbados for the past many months. My table companions asked about the subject of my work, and I explained that I was working on a book about Archbishop Granville Williams and the Barbados Spiritual Baptists. I was surprised by the vitriolic retort that followed from one of the people at the table. She said that Williams was a trickster and that the Spiritual Baptists practised Voodoo. In a time-honoured Barbadian turn of phrase, she stated that she didn't know what was worth studying about those people. The classic Bajan (the diminutive form of Barbadian) reference to "those people" was a distancing manoeuvre. She was not one of them and she had made that clear.

Our attention then was on the Spiritual Baptists' "mourning" ceremony. I learned a long time ago that, during any Barbadian discussion about the Spiritual Baptists, the topic of mourning will come up. My friend did not disappoint me. She had been informed about the "mourning ground" and she'd heard that during mourning, a sheet is used, under which one can find Williams and the women who are mourning. In this apparently simple observation was, of course, the thinly veiled allusion to coerced sexual practices led by Williams. She next concluded her argument by making the pronouncement that the group was nothing but a cult. By the set of my friend's jaw, her flashing eyes and mocking half-smile, I knew she didn't mean by "cult" that the Spiritual Baptists constituted a new religious movement. She was dismissing me with her view that the group was playing at religion, using religious ritual to cover up other intentions.

I was taken aback by the comments, as it had been a long time since I had heard such concentrated criticism being spoken about Williams and the Spiritual Baptists in Barbados. Furthermore, information gleaned from the interviews I conducted between 2007 and 2009 demonstrated that the public's views of the group had dramatically changed. And when I interviewed pastors from other Barbadian denominations, the findings were just as striking and made clear that it was reasonable to conclude that the Church is now enjoying a respected and accepted status (Griffith, Mahy and Young 2008).

At the dinner table, I rapidly reviewed those results, which only provoked greater ire from my table companion. She began then to malign my informants to emphasize that I was not about to dissuade her from the stances she had already taken. From then on, we were no longer on the same wavelength and we couldn't hear each other. Given the surprising negativity of all that she had to say, I finally asked whether she'd ever been to church at one of the Spiritual Baptist temples or whether she knew Archbishop Williams. I decided that I had to know that much before closing the conversation or changing the subject. It turned out that her only attendance at the temple was on an occasion when she had been to a funeral. Not surprisingly, she had also never had personal dealings with the Archbishop. She was aware, however, that he had brought this "strange" religion from Trinidad, a theme that I have come to recognize easily after years of studying the Spiritual Baptist Church: the connection in the minds of Barbadians between Trinidad and religion usually leads to a negative conclusion.

Still, I could not ignore what I had heard in this conversation. It made me think about how difficult things must have been for Williams and his converts in the early years of the movement, and I was reminded again that the prejudices of Barbadians against these foreign ideas were indeed solidly rooted. But as I turned over this conversation in my mind I began to gain some perspective. I contemplated some of the elements that might have initially fuelled all the hostile speculation about Granville Williams. For example, if one happened to see him for the first time in a cotton robe tightened at the waist with a sash or belt, wearing sandals or going without shoes, and with his head encircled by a towel or covered by a simple skullcap, I could understand that the image might give pause. It would not have been the way pastors were attired in Barbados during the late 1950s. But that was precisely his attire on the evening of Maundy Thursday in 2007, as he set about to wash the feet of his parishioners and to anoint them with oil. When he is dressed like that, any conservative, churchgoing Barbadian is likely to raise his eyebrows in wonderment.

Another friend has pointed out to me a second unnerving characteristic of the Archbishop: his eyes. Both of them do not seem to move together to produce what medical men would call conjugate gaze. Rather, they seem to have a degree of independent movement that makes it difficult for bystanders to be sure of the direction of his attention. In addition, his eyes are not large. When these physical attributes are added to his tendency to close his eyes in contemplation at moments he is in conversation with you, it is easy to grasp why some individuals jump to the conclusion that he may have special powers. Informants have explained to me their ideas about the relationship between eyes and the spirit world. Granville Williams habitually appears to look beyond those who are in front of him. It suggests that material things in our physical universe do not consume all his interest. He is capable of looking beyond all this and having his senses fixed on higher planes. I understand that the Archbishop's eyes inspire fear in some and respect in most of those with whom he must interact. His ready smile and gentle charm also cause disarray in those who are fascinated by his impenetrable gaze.

I have sometimes had the impression that the Archbishop enjoys having this effect on people. I have thought, too, that he recognizes in some way the power of his impact on others and that his overall effect is reinforced by the manner that he has cultivated in these interactions, especially with outsiders. He often answers his telephone with a simple "Peace!" Then he patiently waits for the caller to identify himself and announce his business. He has the disconcerting habit of answering questions with an uncomplicated, declarative sentence that leaves it up to you to ponder the content of his statement and decide what you will say next. This capacity to tolerate silence and to carry on unrushed conversations contributes to the mystique that surrounds his persona. It makes him seem an unruffled, peaceful man of God. And for those who are inclined to be fearful when they recognize these traits in any one person, he seems the embodiment of a spiritual man, whatever such an individual must look like.

These allusions to physical spirituality are at first puzzling. But their persistence in the folklore of Barbados caused me to look for other evidence that could conceivably support these claims, and I saw some data emerge in my discussions with one of my interviewees. Full appreciation of what that individual explained to me, however, requires an understanding of the role that the supernatural may play in the Caribbean. This individual dreamt that he was in the middle of a ceremony and was following a procession of Spiritual Baptists. He wanted to speak, but, before doing so, a man who looked like Leader Williams instructed him that he first had to pick a flower. My informant complied with this requirement, which immediately caused his clothing to be transformed into a long, white robe with a red sash. The Leader then invited the informant to follow him. The informant refused, and the Leader replied, "Soon, soon." At that, my informant woke up.

This dream prompted him to find out more about the Spiritual Baptists. So he went to the Church some days after having had the dream. As he watched the proceedings, Williams came toward him and asked him about the dream, intimating that he knew all about it. Since the informant was confident that he had told no one about his dream, Williams's questions worried him, and the informant left the service, frightened by the Leader's apparent mystical ability to see such things. The individual went back to another service at the Church and eventually joined the group. It is this kind of story that impresses some and frightens others as Williams's spiritual powers are discussed. These stories also remind us of Paton's (2009) observations and make clear that we can find relics of the persistent Barbadian fear of Obeah in the most unlikely of places. And when my friend spoke of Williams's involvement with Voodoo, it was a generic reference to Obeah. These minor stories, told in a negative context, also reaffirm the notion that there will be no legitimization of Orisha activity in Barbados, at least in the foreseeable future, as Henry (2003) has described as taking place in Trinidad.

There are aspects of peacefulness and contentment in Williams's demeanour, reinforced by some of his habits, such as his style of entering the Church while the congregation is singing or praying. He proceeds to the middle of the sanctuary and simply stands there with his arms clasped behind his back as he surveys what preparations have been carried out. Then he quietly turns his body a full three hundred sixty degrees without saying a single word. One night when he had carried out this review yet another time, however, he was displeased. He summoned a woman and said something to her, obviously indicating his displeasure and stating that some preparation should be redone. From my position, at some yards from where this exchange was taking place, I got the impression that the hapless woman was defending herself and explaining why things had turned out the way they had. The Archbishop's gruff reply was carried to the pew in which I was sitting. I could hear him say, "Those were not the instructions I gave to you." His words communicated his unmistakable irritation, which suggested that his trust in her had been misplaced. He made clear that his instructions on certain matters should not be reinterpreted or creatively transformed; her task was to do as she was told. Over the years I have not seen this flash of irritability often, but seeing it once was enough to know that its potential is there in this man. Understanding it fully was to see the dejection that set in on the face of the woman who felt the force of his displeasure. In his anger, he had inflicted pain. But it had not been done with drama and shouting. He had proceeded with the icy calm that a leader, one who is confident of his position and accomplishments, can display at the times when his will has been thwarted.

As expected in leaders who have complex personalities, Williams's fastidiousness and his meticulous attention to detail are also traits that have won him plaudits from among many of his followers. Informants who know him well speak highly of his unwillingness to suffer fools gladly. He expects adherence to the traditional Barbadian qualities of promptness, civility, quietness, respect and industry. At the same time, he wears the thin skin of Barbadian men who have worked hard to reach the top. Just underneath the surface is a cauldron that can boil over when stress reaches a level that seems to threaten the equilibrium that carries him through from one day to the next.

Williams's irritability must also have erupted on the occasion a number of years ago when he and a group from his congregation were travelling in the Grenadines. I was not there, but several Church members mentioned it to me. The group was going from island to island, and two members missed the boat and had to spend a night or two separated from the Archbishop and his core travellers. When the boat passed back and the stray travellers rejoined the team, they were welcomed with corporal punishment that was administered by the Archbishop in front of the group. Williams's behaviour on this occasion contradicted my impression that he was forever calm and serene. But he explained to me that the members who had missed the boat had committed a serious infraction and, as a result, had to be punished. He also made no effort to conceal the fact that, at the time, he was very angry and also quite concerned about their welfare. He added, too, that the Holy Spirit had dictated to him that the punishment be administered, and he was obligated to follow the spiritual commandment. Most of those I interviewed about the incident supported the Archbishop and added, to my surprise, that corporal punishment for serious infractions was a tradition among the Spiritual Baptists. Henney (1982) has documented this practice among the Spiritual Baptists in St Vincent. The right of Spiritual Baptist Leaders to administer corporal punishment seems linked to the complex notion that Leaders are spiritual fathers entrusted with the onerous burden of leading their flock along the straight spiritual path.

In the years since the flogging incident occurred, no one can recall anything similar. It seems clear therefore that the frequency of such infractions is rare among the group. And as Williams explained, refusal to submit to the punishment would have meant that the transgressors would have had to give up their group membership. A few other members, however, stated that they would not consent to such punishment. It was also their view that these things happen to young people, not to older folk in the Church. They doubted that the Archbishop would have done it to a woman who was married and had a husband to defend her.

More commonly observable is the manifesting of Williams's authority in quiet, almost imperceptible ways. At one church service that took place just outside Boston, Massachusetts, for example, it was prayer time. Members of the congregation were taking turns leading the church in prayer. It was a day of celebration, and several churches were worshipping together. It is natural for a number of people to seize this opportunity to be visible in the ceremony, so the praying was taking up time. The Archbishop stepped forward and made himself the unofficial timekeeper. Each time a new person took a turn leading prayer at the prayer stool, Williams simply put his hand on the shoulder of the prayer leader and, at the point he judged appropriate, squeezed. The prayer leader would then seem to lose steam and would close out his or her turn at the prayer stool. As a result of Williams's intervention, the prayer session took on a greater sense of orderliness, and each individual used the time as prayer leader more economically and efficiently. It was an impressive display of the Archbishop's being in command of the troops, while still displaying his leadership with a tranquil solicitude for the self-esteem of those who are under his care.

One individual I interviewed described a vignette from another service and showed me the audio-visual clip that had captured the entire scene. In it I could tell that a service was going on in a church in New York City. This church utilized a portable centre-pole in the form of a wheel. Apparently, a woman local to the New York church was in charge of the pole and its attached wheel, but a visitor from the Archbishop's Church touched the pole and spun the wheel. Presumably, the visitor had asserted her spiritual authority to touch the wheel, and the host had questioned the validity of the visitor's claim. A struggle then ensued, as is quite evident in the film clip. Both women had their hands on the wheel and were competing for spiritual dominance in the control of the wheel. Neither would give up. Finally, the Archbishop approached the women, placed his hands on the wheel and quietly prevented its further movement. When the tugging on the wheel had stopped, he then appeared to bless each woman quietly, and both women eventually took their hands off the sacred implement and left things alone. The Archbishop had imposed his authority without uttering a single word. His was the final decision. Of interest, too, is that, while the whole transaction was taking place, the congregation was singing and carrying on the service. The observers, the witnesses to this spiritual contretemps, were unfazed. They were comfortable. Their leader was there on the scene, and the matter was resolved with the intervention of their Archbishop. I would hear it said many times during my visits to the services, "Granville Williams is a man of God." And, indeed, it would be said as much by those who had been with him from the time of his 1957 arrival in Barbados, as it would be uttered by those who had known him only a couple of years. Each time I heard it, I was impressed by the conviction and commitment of the speaker to the truth of the matter. Nevertheless, it is not easy to categorize Granville Williams. He is a man of many parts, with a multifaceted personality that is viewed differently by different observers.

In the time that I have known him, Granville Williams has become more open in discussing his wishes for the future, particularly as they relate to the longitudinal maturation of the Spiritual Baptist Church in Barbados. The architectural expansion of the building at Ealing Grove, Christ Church, is evident. The Church at Zion is now clearly secondary, as Ealing Grove has taken on massive proportions. A third Church built in St Lucy's parish is now temporarily closed and undergoing repairs. This latter facility is far from the other two, and it is not clear that a local congregation exists to support the St Lucy

Figure 9.1 New building being constructed in Ealing Grove, Christ Church. Barbados, 2008.

initiative. But Williams wants to continue expanding the principal Church at Ealing Grove, which has been named a cathedral and is surrounded by a number of imposing buildings that will house apartments and perhaps a senior citizens' home, in addition to a restaurant.

Most intriguing is his wish to build a monastery and convent that will concentrate on the training of Spiritual Baptist ministers and other religious officials. Such an activity, if realized, would constitute a bold move to transform the training of the Spiritual Baptist clergy from a largely informal process into a formalized and structured educational experience. This development would have an effect that would last years and obviously disadvantage those who seek office among the Spiritual Baptist clergy even though they have but a modicum of formal educational preparation. But the advantages are evident to observers. The most obvious one is that these changes will help cement the place of the Spiritual Baptist movement in the mainstream of Caribbean religious denominations. Such a move is already afoot, as evidenced by Williams's appointment in September 2008 as Patriarch for the Jurisdiction of Barbados within the Spiritual Baptist faith. The establishment of a Patriarchate to run the Spiritual Baptist group throughout the Caribbean and North America makes a bold statement about both the future organization and leadership of the movement. It also makes transparent that Granville Williams is seen by his peers as a true Leader in the movement. The following was said about him on the occasion of his installation as a member of the Patriarchate:

> Archbishop Granville Williams began his ministry back in 1945 in Trinidad when the Spiritual Baptist religion, so peculiar to man[,] was illegal in the twin island republic.
>
> He was later very instrumental in the repealing of the Shouters Prohibition Ordinance on March 30, 1951, having walked on Red House in Trinidad as a member of the West Indian Ecclesiastical Spiritual Baptist faith.
>
> He subsequently relocated to his homeland Barbados in 1957, which resulted in the Sons of God Apostolic Spiritual Baptist faith's coming into being and transforming Barbados from a society stagnant in its Eurocentric religious beliefs, to one oriented to suit the vast Afro-Barbadian population.
>
> Archbishop Williams remains adamant that the Spiritual Baptist religion in Barbados remains unrepentant in its philosophical position regarding Africa and Africans, but is equally adamant against racism and prejudice of any form.
>
> Over the last 50 years, the Spiritual Baptist religion, under the guidance of Arch-

bishop Williams has endeared itself to the Barbadian public. This is evident in the group's participation in festivals such as the national celebrations of Crop Over, NIFCA and CARIFESTA, as well as through village fairs, concerts, and the annual "By Way of Radio Spiritual Baptist" programme.

He also endeared the society with the unprecedented public observance of the faith's ceremonial rituals of Harvests, its Nation Feasts, Baptisms, and Palm Sunday and Good Friday's street processions that would regularly draw tremendous street crowds.

Archbishop Granville Williams is a Justice of the Peace. He received the Barbados Centennial Honors in 2001. He currently sits on the Religious Advisory Committee on National Affairs. Having garnered the distinction as an iconic historical figure in the Barbados society, the Spiritual Baptist faith which he leads there, occupies a distinctive place in the Barbados religious community, and as the nation's only indigenous religion.

He has carried out a lecture-tour of black studies departments at the University of Massachusetts at Amherst, Smith College, Amherst College, Mount Holyoke College and Hampshire College where he spoke on Barbadian Folk Culture. Williams also toured Yale University, Trinity College, Columbia University, Hunter College, the State University of New York at Buffalo and Howard University where he spoke on Bajan Folklore and the function of the Spiritual Baptist faith within the Barbadian Society.

Archbishop Williams's legacy encompasses what will probably come to be known as the eighth wonder of the world—the preeminent Cathedral Church of Jerusalem at Ealing Grove, Christ Church, Barbados. When completed, it will feature a senior citizens' home, apartments, restaurant, administration office, nursery, cathedral shop, monastery and convent.

The Archbishop has traveled extensively through the United States, Canada, Europe and the Caribbean. Earlier this year he followed the steps of Moses and led a pilgrimage to the Holy Land—from the Great Pyramids to Mount Sinai, the Red Sea and the Nile; from Mount Nebo to Capernaum; from Mount Carmel to the Garden of Gethsemane; from Mount Zion to the Upper Room; from Caesarea to Tabgha, the site of the multiplication of the loaves and fishes; from the Jordan River to our own sandy shore, where Rachel laps at our feet.

Archbishop Williams is the recipient of numerous honours, citations, and awards. His superb leadership in transforming the Barbadian society from an entrenched Anglo-Saxon religious one to an Afrocentric indigenous religious society has earned him international recognition as a religious force. He has influenced cultural thinking in Caribbean society, and his faithfulness in ministry for over fifty years has earned

> him the respect of his peers and, by unanimous vote, election to the *Apostolic Patriarchate.* (Spiritual Baptist Church 2008)

No doubt in recognition of his advancing age and of the achievements of those he has trained over the last five decades, Archbishop Williams consecrated two Bishops in Barbados on 23 December 2007. This is reassuring evidence to many in his congregation that he has begun to give thought to his succession, although many members have pointed out to me that the final choice will be the Holy Spirit's decision (a reminder that it is a unique part of Spiritual Baptist orthodoxy to insist that important administrative decisions in the Church are made by the Holy Spirit). Williams has consistently been very reticent about his wishes or plans for the future. He generally avoids my gentle probing by saying that the Holy Spirit will take care of things. That may very well be the case for those who subscribe to Spiritual Baptist theology. Others will take heart from the insidious appearance of greater organization in the Church and recognize that the group is preparing for the future. In his own characteristically indirect way, the Archbishop obliquely acknowledges that the world continues to change. To keep pace with the changes and remain strong, the movement that he has built over the last fifty years must take on some of the trappings of other, more sophisticated organizations. Even he knows that just maintaining the impressive buildings he has had constructed will require monitoring so as to forestall the deterioration caused by the sun and sea-spray in Barbados. Their theological use will demand serious oversight as well. And, of course, everything will require structured financial planning. This is now an obvious imperative, especially since all my informants (members and non-members alike) agree that what the Archbishop has built is now considered a major and unparalleled achievement among churches in the English-speaking Caribbean.

The road to permanency is, for most organizations, paved with challenges and difficulties, and several recent events have demonstrated this clearly for the Barbados Spiritual Baptists. In August 2008, just after the Church's Cou Cou Village restaurant had been a smashing success at that year's national Crop Over Festival, the restaurant's receipts were stolen (Slinger 2008). The theft occurred literally minutes after the money, reported to be thousands of Barbadian dollars, had been counted in a secluded room of the Church. The loss of the money has been a financial nightmare for the group, as the preparation and work that went into the entire production were significant. Indeed, few church groups anywhere in the Caribbean can afford to lose substantial amounts of money. Of additional import in relation to this incident has been the recognition by several members whom I interviewed that the theft may have been carried out by someone who knew the Church well – as benign a way as possible of saying that it was likely a member who stole the money.

Figure 9.2 Bishop Malcolm Babb, one of the two Bishops consecrated in 2007. Jerusalem Cathedral, Barbados, 2009. (Photo by Felix Kerr.)

Put in other words, of course, someone betrayed the Archbishop and the other members who had worked so hard to make the Church restaurant a hit at the national celebration. The act of deceit undermined the Leader's accomplishments and weakened his call to the members to live their lives at every turn in tune with the Holy Spirit. Of course, this assertion must be an exaggeration, as the leadership of no religious group should be held responsible for every action carried out by its members. Even so, most church leaders are stung when trickery is carried out against them by their own followers. What is worse is that the occurrence of this incident at such a crucial point in the Church's history suggests a certain vulnerability of the organization because it makes members wonder who could have had the courage to commit such a crime against the Archbishop and the group.

The Leader conceded to me that he has not effectively pursued security around the Church's premises so as to prevent this kind of negative event.

Once I realized that other thefts of the Church's money had taken place in the past, it seemed a legitimate consideration that he had not learned from past experiences of this nature. There is no doubt that, in matters of Church administration, the Archbishop is very experienced. Consequently, I have theorized that his failure to stem the recurrence of these thefts is related to his hope that the guilty parties will eventually understand they are stealing goods from the Master's house. As a result, they will have to face the music eventually, and the reckoning will be with God directly. In addition, I suspect that the Leader is not enamoured of the idea that he might one day be giving evidence in a court of law against one of his own members. The publicity would be scandalous and make tongues wag throughout the entire Caribbean.

The significance of this act cannot be emphasized enough; it has taken on the peculiar standing of an event in the life of the Church. I was somewhat surprised, too, when I learned that a few members had had a vision, a premonition, that the theft would take place. Consequently, some members remained puzzled and even angry that the Leader had not taken steps to prevent the loss. After all, it is a stain on the organization and has clearly dampened the spirits of the members.

Another event of similar proportions occurred early in 2009. A letter, obviously written by an upset and discontented member (or members) of the Church, was circulated to a number of people in the group. The missive provoked enough concern to cause it to be read aloud at a general meeting of the Church. In this way, it became a public document, and the Leader could confront it openly. Nevertheless, its contents, apparently detailing a number of complaints about the Leader in straightforward terms, have caused so much consternation that, in response to my inquiries, members gave limited responses. Many said that they were not on the distribution list and therefore could not make appropriate comments about a letter they had not read. Others simply preferred to have me talk directly to the Leader about the matter, fearing that their discussing the matter with me would leave them tainted in some way. I think it fairly clear that they did not wish to be identified by anyone, especially by the Leader, as participants in this tempest.

My discussions with the Leader about the letter have not been particularly expansive. He seemed preoccupied, however, with the idea that there are people in the Church who want to sow strife and cause the kind of disharmony that might lead to a disintegration of the Church. Spiritual Baptist members are not expected to air their linen so publicly and disrespectfully, and this has caused the Leader considerable personal pain. He labelled the missive a letter of hate and disgrace, and, try as he might, it was hard for him to see the event as anything but a personal attack on his leadership and his accomplishments. Leaders in the Spiritual Baptist faith are not accustomed to being challenged in this formalized way by their own members' written articulation of complaints and public dissemination of grievances. So it is not surprising that the Archbishop was upset by this affront to his leadership. The important question now, of course, involves the depth of his distress. Matters of this sort always evoke in the leaders of organizations the peculiar sensation that the complaints have arisen from some fundamental flaw in the administrative style of those in charge. The feeling is often not acknowledged directly, but it is my belief that it is partly responsible for leaders' uneasiness, and that this is typically the case even as those in charge go about systematically defending themselves against the charges mounted by their underlings.

A few months after the offending letter had been circulated, I attended a prayer service at the Church. The service was held on the evening of a weekday, with a relative handful of people present. After the introductory prayers and Bible readings were completed, the service was then turned over to the Archbishop. He promptly took to task the few faithful present and started talking about their wanting to behave "as they like" and to be undisciplined in the sight of God. I couldn't help thinking that there was a certain irritability about him as he upbraided the members present. I noted to myself that I had seen him in this mood before. But then he mentioned, in a stream-of-consciousness way, that there were people trying to break up the Church. And those individuals were solid examples of the undisciplined who wanted to proceed to do as they liked. At that point, I couldn't help but think that there was indeed a connection between his irritability and the letter. He even brought up the fact that he had made the decision not to attend the usual Spiritual Baptist celebrations in Trinidad that mark, at the end of every March, the removal of that island's prohibition against the Spiritual Baptist faith. He had taken that decision because he had judged it unwise to be absent from the Church for a week at a time of discontent among his members. Toward the end of this mini-lecture, as it was not an affirming type of sermon, he surprised me by mentioning that he was growing old and would not be around forever, and that he wanted to leave the Church functioning in an orderly, disciplined fashion.

This was the first time I had heard him mention his possible death, and I was taken aback. As I thought further about all that he was going through, I surmised that he was confronting the changes in society around him that were impinging on his Church, the one he had founded over fifty years ago, and the going was a bit rocky. But he found his equilibrium once again, and he started talking about his plans for the future. He discussed his projected trip to the United States in May 2009, when he would help celebrate the anniversaries of the founding of churches in Massachusetts and New York. Those churches were started by members who had emigrated from Barbados, and who were his spiritual sons. It must have been reassuring to him that his labour had increased and multiplied his flock, palpable proof that his view of things over the years has been reviewed and blessed from above. He also talked about his plan to take a trip in 2010 to visit the biblical churches of Asia, which suggested that he simultaneously had a positive way of framing the future. In fact, the planned 2009 trip to the United States did not take place. Its cancellation was said to be the result of the swine flu epidemic then troubling the American population. But I was not convinced by this explanation.

Figure 9.3 Worship service at the Scarlet Cord Apostolic Spiritual Baptist Temple. New Bedford, Massachusetts, May 2008.

Figure 9.4 Façade of the Bethlehem Sons of God Apostolic Spiritual Baptist Church. Brooklyn, New York, July 2008.

In this light, to me as an observer, the dissidents in Williams's Church seemed to be upstarts. But it didn't take much sustained reflection to recognize that this light was being focused by the Archbishop himself. He was making the point, lucidly and unambiguously, that the dissidents were provocateurs seeking to cause confusion, to provoke discord and alienation. He was intent on keeping the disarray contained, to safeguard his authority, to maintain his Church strong, to protect the future of what he had built and to fulfil his commitment to God that he would keep his Church members on the straight and narrow path and prepare them well for judgement day. Other members supportive of the Archbishop, even as they remained temperate in their comments, saw the letter as representative of Satan's doings. The letter was a sign of jealousy and envy and a reflection that some members had stopped praying and worshipping truthfully.

The objective of containing members' discontent and protecting the Church's future is not as easy to complete as one might think. I realized this when my attention was drawn to a trial that recently took place in the Church. The point here is not to delve into the minute details of the matter or to determine who was right and who was wrong, but to draw principles from it that might clarify what was transpiring within the Church in 2009. After all, I was witnessing these events as they unfolded, although I was never simultaneously privy to all that was happening. In addition, I recognized that I needed interpreters. Nothing I saw was an event really starting *de novo*. In each case there had been a preamble about which I knew little or nothing. I usually failed to appreciate immediately who was on which side in Church disputes, but with patient probing I learned to decipher the different strains of partisanship running through my many informants. I also decided that every participant in the conflict fervently believed that, in Spiritual Baptist affairs and disputes, God was on his side. I shall no doubt repeat this maxim, as it is probably the most profound impediment to the facile resolution of the disagreements.

It was reported to me that, in this recent case, someone had made Leader Williams aware of alleged transgressions committed by a Church member, who was then summoned to an evening meeting at which his actions were reviewed. It was stated that the Archbishop conducted this hearing as plaintiff and judge, and described the respondent as wicked and demon-possessed. Apparently, the respondent and other supporters objected to the complaints that had been lodged against the respondent and subsequently prosecuted by the Archbishop, who refused to identify the source of his information or to produce witnesses. Archbishop Williams preferred instead to focus on the alleged infractions. But the respondent insisted that it was an abuse of form to have to answer charges brought by invisible complainants. Not surprisingly, the Leader saw the respondent's defence as the demonstration of a lack of respect for authority, and apparently proceeded to reach some conclusion about the kind of punishment due in such a case. It seems that, as things progressed, the respondent's insistence on a right of due process got transformed into a further manifestation of unruliness and lack of respect for leadership and discipline.

Leader Williams gave me a different explanation of the trial, which was corroborated by a number of members who had firsthand information about the matter. In discussing this incident with Church informants, it quickly became obvious that everyone, even though each person said relatively little about the matter, had reached a partisan position about what had transpired.

In fact, it remained unclear to me what the precise conclusion to the trial was. There was, however, no lack of clarity about the notions that the respondent had been demeaned and humbled by the hearing itself, and that the incident had provoked polarization in the Church. Of course, each side was confident of the inherent rightness of its opinions and also believed, with unconventional stubbornness, that, as I have said before, God was on its side.

Without attending to the gravity of the allegations and having no knowledge of their truthfulness, it appeared to me that Archbishop Williams and one of his members were struggling over a matter that, to the Archbishop, was yet another assault on his preeminent authority over the organization that he founded and developed. The respondent was obviously better educated than Church members of a bygone time, and the Archbishop could hardly be expected to see the respondent's insistence on procedural fairness as other than an affront and a challenge to the organization's Leader. In addition, Williams had to have been aware of the grumbling that the respondent was being railroaded, which doubtless made it seem, in turn, that the respondent had a hand in fomenting the unruliness that seemed to be cropping up here and there within the Church. It was not the state of affairs that would warm the heart of a Leader, now in the last years of his eighth decade, who has been accustomed to having his way over the last fifty years in running his Church. Things were not helped either by Williams's own recognition that some members were openly talking about his advancing age. Of course, the record should be clear that other members were in disagreement with the respondent and maintained that the Leader had for years been patient with the respondent and had overlooked many of the individual's earlier transgressions.

I see the significance of this trial for the life of the group as flowing from its proximate relationship to both the theft and the letter. These events were fairly close together in time and have taken a toll on the energy of the Leader and of the Church's membership. Such occurrences are not in themselves unusual or unheard of in religious organizations, but in this particular Church, in which the Leader needs space and time to implement his plans, these disruptive events shattered the tranquillity and concentration necessary for effective long-term planning.

As I sat in a service on an overcast Sunday morning in March 2009, I wondered about the heavy burdens facing Archbishop Williams. That particular day he was energetic and he preached a fairly long sermon, although some may not have recognized it as such, since he was talking with microphone in hand as he moved about the floor of the Church. Suddenly his irritability took hold and he began explicitly to berate a member. The Archbishop described his displeasure with the member in question and then forbade the member and family from taking part in certain Church activities. In other words, they were put on the proverbial backbench. This punishment was to stay in place until the Archbishop was persuaded that the entire family's behaviour had changed. Unaccustomed to the public airing of these pronouncements and edicts, I was caught off guard by Williams's action. Other members explained after the service that the Archbishop's behaviour was not unusual, at least not in the context of a Spiritual Baptist church. One informant made clear that this cleaning process was essential to the invigorated rebirth of this Church.

I found it hard, however, to escape my reflections about the mental health status of those who are the objects of such a public correction. There seemed to be little compassion in the process, and I felt confident that the family members concerned would experience the rebuke as traumatic. The object of the Archbishop's criticism stood there and took the punishment without saying a word. The member was not even asked to speak, or to offer anything in self-defence. The member had lost all voice, all capacity to witness on behalf of self. And no other member spoke up in support. What I also found disconcerting was that this incident unfolded in the midst of a service, enveloped in hymns and prayers. The conclusion was that the lifting of the punishment would be at the pleasure of the Leader, a hearkening back to judicial processes of old when the lifting of certain punishments would be at the pleasure of the monarch. Furthermore, as usual, the Archbishop couched his edicts, harshness and all, as necessary in the sight of God.

I did not, at first, grasp the connection between this incident and the trial of a few weeks earlier. But, once it was explained to me by knowledgeable sources, I recognized the interconnectedness of the events of the last few months. It all seemed to confirm my theory that the Leader was under considerable stress, and that he was responding to the perceived disruption of the traditional Spiritual Baptist way. He wanted to quell the uprising with a heavy hand, directed by the Holy Spirit. As he did so, he was encountering a rebelliousness that I could predict would easily come. The dissidents were insisting that the Church's leadership incorporate signs of modernity, such as fairness, dignity, respect for others and justice. The Archbishop and his supporters recast all of these demands as the manifestation of evidence of a creeping sense of ungodliness. They met the onslaught with increased rigidity and a stringent call for a return to the origins of the Spiritual Baptist faith, one that was rooted in Old Testament orthodoxy and the notion that Church members should be humble and, yes, obedient to authority.

It was a theory that I was turning over in my mind, at least. Then, in a later discussion with a Church member, an overt supporter of Archbishop Williams, I was urged to consider the entire dispute in a biblical context and was referred to the story of Korah, a biblical figure who was unfamiliar to me. I found Korah and his activities in Numbers 16. It turned out that Korah and other members of the Israelite assembly had "gathered themselves together against Moses and against Aaron" (Numbers 16:3). Moses was, of course, angry at the uprising and took his case to the Lord, who supported Moses and, in turn, punished the rebellious group by swallowing them up in an open pit. Moses took pains to point out that the harsh punishment was not meted out by him but by God. His explanation was not convincing, and the Israelites murmured their disapproval of the deaths of Korah and his group. This persistent strife continued to anger the Lord, and He then punished the group with a plague that was stayed by the pleading of Moses.

The story is complex. Reading it several times, I ultimately grasped the idea that Korah's group saw Moses as seeking his own aggrandizement in the way he carried out his leadership chores. This is what Spiritual Baptists call "seeking your own glory". In turn, Moses accused Korah and his group of being dissatisfied with what the Lord had asked them to do in the service of His tabernacle, and surmised that they wanted to be a formal part of the priesthood – to receive a promotion, in other words. Then Moses pointedly asked them, without saying more, what Aaron, the leader of the priesthood, had done to deserve their criticism.

My informant had hit the nail squarely on the head with the reference to this narrative. Korah and Moses were both persuaded of the rightness of their causes, even as they opposed each other. Neither one could own up to any personal ambition, pride or unusual interest in the outcome of the arguments. Ultimately, the justness of the outcome was based on God's judgement. But God's reasoning was inscrutable to the masses and dependent on a faith-based understanding of His commitment to those He had placed in charge. My informant saw Archbishop Williams as a modern-day Moses forced to cope with the insurgency of a group of people driven by their own personal ambitions and desires. The informant was also confident that these people would be punished by God.

In reviewing this symbolic biblical story with a Pentecostal minister in Barbados, she insisted that the fundamental point in the narrative is that Moses was God's man. Consequently, Korah was not kicking against Moses, but against God. Furthermore, she argued, Korah must have seen how God had been guiding Moses and must have witnessed what God had done for the group through Moses, who was His instrument. This minister went on to make a point that I had not previously considered – that Moses' successes under God's guidance ultimately blinded him somewhat and he, in turn, made his own mistakes and did not see the Promised Land. Even if this interpretation is the minister's idiosyncratic view of the biblical narrative, it is still useful to contemplate her conclusions and to recognize the difficulty in bringing together warring factions in a church setting.

I was fortunate to discuss the events of the trial with informants who were on the side of the person against whom the complaints had been lodged. They emphasized that the accused member had not been accorded the opportunity for self-defence. The individual had not really been permitted even to speak and to self-represent. Just as a partisan defender of Archbishop Williams had sent me to search out the story of Korah, a supporter of the respondent in the affair reminded me that, even when Paul went to Agrippa, Paul was given the chance to speak (Acts 25 and 26). The story referred to recounts the occasion when Paul was held prisoner and was told that it was reasonable for him to know the charges pending against him. He was then given permission to speak for himself. Acts 26:1 states that "Agrippa said to Paul, 'You have permission to speak for yourself.' Then Paul stretched out his hand and spoke for himself." In a poignant conclusion to his account, the respondent's supporter said, with profound sadness, that the Archbishop always states that God has sent him. But the informant argued that God never said that the Archbishop should take advantage of Church members.

An Anglican priest gave me his unique view on this argument. He suggested that the two principal concepts in operation here are the notion of spiritual authority and that of ecclesiastical authority. I appreciated this insight, as it helped me to see more clearly how Archbishop Williams could persistently argue that the respondent and supporters were irrelevantly introducing concepts of procedural fairness, for example. The Leader emphasized his own rightness, which was rooted in God's call to him to lead his flock in righteousness and almost rigid perfection. Hence, he could not be overruled by rules invented by man, all of which were extraneous to the laws of God. At the same time, the respondent and supporters, well educated and now thoroughly schooled in secular claims to authority, saw that Leader Williams, as head of the Church, was invoking ecclesiastical authority – which is to say that he was calling on authority that derived from the Church as an organized institution. In that case, he could not simply discard notions of fairness that were established points of reference in secular Barbados.

Most telling about all this was the sharp insights that the struggles provided about the Archbishop and his relationship with his congregation. His own success in building his Church had created a new following, characterized by thoughtfulness and a capacity to raise questions in ways that would not have been imaginable in years gone by. The Anglican priest's point was that spirituality as a guiding principle tends to work better in small groups that are protected from reliance on secular concepts. As the group gets larger, better educated and familiar with secular organizational ideas, leadership becomes a more complicated undertaking. Needless to say, several Church members with whom I discussed these ideas returned inevitably to the point that the Archbishop, in growing steadily older, is naturally more resistant to this complexity. He cannot be expected to embrace such change.

My own wish was that a resolution of the matter would come quickly. I wondered whether anyone among the Church's members had the spiritual standing to act as an intermediary and to solve things so that the stress level in the Church could diminish and be replaced by functional cohesiveness. After all, a resolution needed to occur so that the entire group could refocus its energies on strategic plans for the future. As I considered this state of affairs further, I recognized the relevance of Seymour's work (2006) to the understanding of the conflict between Williams and a section of his congregation. Seymour notes that the concept of "resistance" has become ubiquitous in cultural anthropology as a framework for contemplating social change and transformation. Picking up on this terminology, I believe it is reasonable to think about Williams's efforts in setting up his Church in Barbados as a study in resistance. Indeed, Williams has made it clear in his own words that he wants to show Afro-Barbadians another way to Christ, one that enhances their blackness and African heritage and affirms their identity as black people. He is also interested in democratizing Church rituals in a way that established churches have never done. As I have stated before, he has successfully introduced this democratic system into the Church, with the exception of his one contradictory idea that male leadership of his Church is obligatorily ordained by biblical ordinance. In this sense, then, Williams has set about to resist the cultural hegemony inherent in the ongoing system of dominance represented by the Anglican Church. He has also linked these religion-based efforts to his stated wish to see a black government one day installed in Barbados. Here he is intermingling concepts of Church and secular politics in his efforts to construct a new identity for Afro-Barbadians, one that will simultaneously have a therapeutic effect. This new identity will be transformative as it enhances the self-esteem of black Barbadians and improves their capacity to function in the secular context.

As novelist Austin Clarke points out at several reprises in *The Polished Hoe* (2002), however, "ironies" are regularly found in Barbadian life. And the role of resistance in the politics of Granville Williams is one important irony worth serious consideration. As Williams polishes his religious ideology and imparts its tenets to his followers, he seems not to count on their internalizing the values of self-respect, fairness, justice and equality. As a result, once disagreements within the group begin, Williams appears to forget that it is he who has taught them how to demand a voice in running their organization, fairness in the resolution of all complaints and how to resist the tendency to give in to subordination of themselves to others.

Regis (2005) has produced an insightful analysis of this type of irony in his work on Eric Williams, a former distinguished prime minister of Trinidad. Regis calls on the musical art form of calypso to make his demonstration lucid. He cites parts of "Get to Hell Out", a 1965 calypso produced by the Mighty Sparrow:

> I defy anyone of you to dictate to me
> I am no dictator
> But when I pass an order
> Mr Speaker, this matter must go no further
> I have nothing more to say
> And it must be done my way . . .

This land is mine
I am the boss
What I say goes
And who vex lorse [lost]

Figure 9.5 Archbishop Granville Williams holding his staff at the service celebrating the fifty-second anniversary of the Church's founding. In the background are members of the Archbishop's Court. Jerusalem Cathedral, Barbados, 2009. (Photo by Felix Kerr.)

The calypso shows a prime minister displaying autocratic tendencies after having exercised considerable leadership of the country in a powerful show of resistance to the entrenched forces of colonialism and white hegemony. But then the prime minister is caught in the same trap, once those he has led turn against him and voice their disagreement. The two lines that are most powerful in this regard are "It must be done my way" and "What I say goes." This language is essentially that of a besieged Granville Williams, who, under pressure, gives in to the impulse to silence critics and to rule autocratically. At least, that is how his opponents see things. Furthermore, the Archbishop's supporters overlook his autocratic behaviour and categorize it as the case of a leader who has rightfully and justifiably lost patience with those who are self-centred and have lost their grounding in God.

CHAPTER 10

Ye Shall Dream

AT SOME POINT IN the 1950s, Granville Williams saw himself being urged in a dream to engage in the missionary task of taking God's word and the Spiritual Baptist faith to his home island of Barbados. Many of us never have such grandiose dreams. Some of us have a dream of one kind or another but never dare to implement it, paralysed by fear and a lack of confidence in confronting the uncertainty of an unconventional future. Others take steps to execute the plans but are then derailed by the anxiety that wells up once some barrier rears its head and grinds the progress temporarily to a halt. But Williams continued, armed with his Bible, lota, bell and the Spiritual Baptist-based capacity to dream dreams and see visions promising success.

He garnered confidence from his dreams and visions, and saw the outcome dictated by a vision in which the Master promised that He would not abandon him. God would not forsake Williams, despite the reality that the way of all missionary adventures is strewn with temptation, false steps, persecution and other unforeseen difficulties. After all, this is what characterized the missionary efforts of Jesus, John the Baptist, Paul and a host of others. So Granville Williams did not and could not expect anything different in his case. But he maintained his tenacity and focus even in the face of warnings from Trinidad that dogs would lick his face in the gutter, and despite the public ridicule that came so strongly from Barbadians in the early years following his return. With all the years that have passed and the many gallons of water that have flowed under the bridge, there is now the inescapable reality that October 2009 represents the fifty-second anniversary of the Church's founding.

Consequently, a special characteristic of this story is that Granville Williams has had the distinctive pleasure of participating in the playing-out of his life's dream over more than a half century. Most of us have to be contented with between twenty-five and thirty-five years as our allotted time with any career ideal. But Williams, more than many others, has been blessed with a long time to work out his life's work. It is also unusual that he has had the benefit of the most unexpected of luxuries: control of the execution of his dream. This is not to suggest that he has been immune to the influence of other factors that usually have some impact on how we live out our dreams, such as money and oppositional opinions. But few of us have the luxury of being the principal architect of how we implement our life's work. He has had unique control of his life's vision for a period of fifty-two years. In distinctly Barbadian and Caribbean terms, Granville Williams has been blessed with a very long time batting at the wicket. He has had the unparalleled freedom to choose his batting strokes, cutting and driving at will, adding flourishes here and there, displaying confidence in his belief that his innings will be successful because his play is ultimately directed by an inner force controlled from above.

Throughout this text, I have worked to present a balanced account of how Patriarch Williams implemented his ideas and set about constructing his Church. I have included stories of his successes and have attempted to put forth fair representations of events that did not bring as much honour to his name. I have also mentioned squarely the opinions of those who have opposed him, especially in recent years. With this in mind, I had no doubt in 2009 that the fifty-second anniversary would be a time of profound celebration. But, as it turned out, it would also be laced with a modicum of bitterness and pain. Only a few days away from the anniversary, one of the Church's Bishops tendered his resignation, sending shockwaves throughout the Church. And as expected, numerous different explanations circulated among the Church's membership.

I have had the occasion to discuss this turn of events with the Patriarch himself. He is hurt, but not surprised. He claims that he saw it all unfold in a dream. He thought at first that Satan was taunting him and trying to trick him into believing that he would be abandoned by several of those close to him. But he finally recognized that events of the past year had come to pass and forced him to confront some of his fears. He claims that he has come to terms with it all, and that he is at peace. He has done the Lord's will and is contented. He reminded me of a vision he had had and pointed out to me the exact physical space at which he had had the experience. He was walking from his house to the Church, and a few feet from the edifice he turned around and saw a dragon. But God appeared and told him not to be afraid. "He cannot harm you," God said – a restatement of His commitment to Williams.

In that same conversation, the Patriarch told me for the first time that, during a service, he had looked toward the back of the Church and had seen honey flowing down the wall. He went and verified it for himself without saying a word to anyone in the Church. The honey was on the inside wall, in exactly the same spot where, on the outside, he had seen God. Looking away from the altar, the spot was at the left corner of the sanctuary. He smiled as he told me about the honey, with his face transcendently radiant. God was giving him yet another sign of their connectedness. And the implication was that, no matter what anyone else did, God would remain on the Patriarch's side, as long as he remained faithful to God's precepts. The Patriarch's faith is therefore solidly rooted in this connection that he believes he has established with his God.

This discussion, taking place as it did only a couple of days before the fifty-second anniversary service, reminded me of the accounts in Joel 2. I saw then more clearly the basis of the Patriarch's reasoning. God expected him to carry out His instructions, to be faithful to His ordinances and to do so in the face of opposition and rebellion. I suddenly realized what Williams meant when he accused members of wanting to do as they liked and of behaving in a ridiculous manner. In the Leader's view, these individuals were trying to circumvent God's rules by appealing to secular ideas and principles, and the Archbishop would have no truck with that. He was not participating in a popularity contest. Neither was he, as he repeated constantly, running a political party. Furthermore, as he explained to me, he had been too liberal, too permissive, and certain Church members had interpreted his lenience as a sign of weakness. So he was back on the path of righteousness, but with reinvigorated tenacity and commitment. And he urged those who wanted to leave the Church to go ahead and do so. This was the natural price of purification and sanctification, of rededication to God's way. Out of this would come an outpouring of God's spirit upon all the faithful members of the Sons of God Apostolic Spiritual Baptist Church of Barbados. Afterwards, as promised in Joel, their sons and daughters would prophesy, their old men would dream dreams and their young men would see visions. Archbishop Williams would not be deterred from his belief in this vision. His Church might be lessened in numbers, but it will not fail. He is confident it will grow stronger again. It is all the price of spiritual renewal.

In the face of the impending anniversary, however, what could be said about what Granville Williams has accomplished since his return to Barbados in 1957? I gave thought to this specific question in discussions with several of my informants. I also reflected on it in the context of frameworks presented by several other authors. One clearly established theme that appeared in these discussions was linked to the Leader's introduction of Afro-Barbadian concepts in his orthodoxy. I refer here to his ideas about the racial definition of Jesus and other biblical personages, his concern specifically about the spiritual condition of black Barbadians and their access to salvation through Jesus Christ, and the earnest belief that black Barbadians could run their own church and develop rituals and practices that were linked to their African heritage. Ownership of their own churches would in turn foster a personal pride in them as black people that could only lead to an enhanced concept of self. This is, of course, what Chatfield (1998) refers to in his comparison of the Caribbean Spiritual Baptist movement with the development of independent churches in Africa. He sees both the African and the Caribbean movements as forms of resistance and struggle against an established social order that was driven by colonialist doctrine and institutions. Archbishop Williams made clear in our discussions that he was aware that the Spiritual Baptist movement represented a form of resistance on two fronts. First, he had been a part of the efforts to overturn the governmental prohibition against the Spiritual Baptist faith in Trinidad. Consequently, he instinctively knew that, in the late 1950s, black Barbadians would not quickly give up their connections to white-established churches and embrace a new Caribbean-based indigenous faith group. He knew he would have to kick against traditions long put in place by churches from overseas. He also understood that the average Afro-Barbadian would not side readily with him in the cultural struggle because Barbadians as a group were too tightly aligned with all that had been dictated to them by their colonial masters. This is, of course, a sharp summary of Williams's thinking in light of Seymour's (2006) theories of resistance.

The second major achievement noted by observers was that, in the face of significant opposition, Williams has pulled off what many initially labelled as impossible. He has built his organization and moved it from being considered a cult, a faith group not to be taken seriously, all the way to a religious organization highly respected in the secular community and recognized by the country's political leadership. This is the Barbadian example of Henry's (2003) concept of the socio-political legitimation of the Caribbean Spiritual Baptist movement. In addition, everyone in the international Spiritual Baptist community knows of Archbishop Granville Williams and his cathedral in Barbados. The older folk and those with an even slight interest in history also know that Williams is one of the few stalwarts left. (This is a disguised reference to his participation in the Trinidad struggle to overturn the government's prohibition against the Spiritual Baptists and his known connection to Archbishop Griffith, who led the opposition in concert with the politician Albert Gomes.) Archbishop Williams has therefore succeeded in helping a cross-section of Barbadians solidify their ethnic and religious identities in a way that reinforces their psychological well-being with hope. They have thrown off their yoke of victimization and have coalesced into a group of considerable distinction and formidable promise.

Williams's initial resistance to the status quo and his ultimate achievement of creating a religious organization built on hope and the functional use of mechanisms such as baptism and mourning have indeed resulted in a distinctive form of a healing community. With their unique rituals, unusual structure, distinctive garments and intriguing symbols, the Barbados Spiritual Baptists have sought to enhance their self-esteem and define their specialized ethnic and religious identities. They have affirmed themselves and displayed performative approaches to distinguishing themselves from other groups while coalescing around their centre-poles and making joyful noises to the Lord with their bells and their prayers.

The one potential problem visible on the horizon after fifty-two years has been the internal bickering developing in the group. But observers with substantial experience in church and organizational development in Barbados told me not to worry about this element. It is common for there to be strife in Barbados churches, and Williams's establishment is not exempt from this tendency. Furthermore, it will only be determined in the future whose position is the correct one. All sides in the disputes will claim to be righteously right, with God at their right hands, and it will be no other way. History will declare the victor. In addition, one seemingly contradictory result – simultaneously ironic and paradoxical – is that the Spiritual Baptist faith in Barbados will benefit. Members will go off and form their own groups, and the faith will multiply. I was told that I had no reason to expect that the Barbados Spiritual Baptists will forever be characterized solely by Granville Williams and the Sons of God Apostolic Spiritual Baptist Church. The story of Korah and the schisms in the early Christian church has made all this clear.

So what future expectations can we have of the Spiritual Baptists in Barbados? Williams and colleagues (Williams, Griffith, Young et al. 1999), and Griffith, Mahy and Young (2008) have suggested a framework for thinking about the development of this ever-growing religious community. It is clear that a major preoccupation of Williams and his entourage in developing and building their Church has been to solidify the economic base, establish the rituals and cement the doctrine that will characterize their faith group. This has been accomplished in spectacular fashion. But their focus has been strongly internal. The authors just mentioned suggest that, in the next phase, Spiritual Baptists will legitimately turn their attention to life outside the Church, especially since so many Barbadians are in need of social and health services that could improve their lives.

For example, in reviewing this subject with members of other faith groups in Barbados, they pointed out that a number of churches were presently involved in different social service programmes: prison ministry, provision of religious education in schools, involvement with residential homes for children, interactive programming in residential facilities for senior citizens, and provision of meals to needy people in the community. These are examples of social service activities that demand the attention of the Spiritual Baptist group, especially now that they have accumulated such trust and respect in secular society. Indeed, some Church members have lamented to me the relative non-use of the wonderful facilities that have been built adjoining the Cathedral at Ealing Grove, where there is now the obvious possibility for use by groups putting on educational symposia and afterschool programmes.

I have discussed this subject with several members at different levels of the organization. They could never explain cogently what constituted impediments to progress in this area. Neither were they sure of the best way to move forward in implementing any ideas that would make the Church a more vibrant participant in the arena of community outreach activities. We could not even discuss fruitfully the role of financial support as a potential catalyst of this genre of activity, as members generally made clear that the financial structure of the Church was apparently known only by the Leader. And he holds those cards very close to the vest. But it will be interesting to watch the next phase of the Church's development. Time will tell whether the Church will remain turned in on itself or will look to serve the broader secular community. No doubt the outcome will depend too on whether the Barbados government sees it as wise to support churches more broadly as useful mechanisms for confronting the needs of the people.

But I would understand if observers made the point to me that it is unreasonable to establish future expectations for this faith group in the face of their present disarray and internal arguments. Some would insist that the bickering must stop and a leadership committee put in place to organize solidly the everyday activities of the Church. That is the first step. Furthermore, it has been repeated to me on numerous occasions by members of the group and also by outsiders that the Church is uniquely constructed on a foundation of spiritual principles that must not be eroded or diluted by the importation of modern administration techniques. I have heard this so often that I understand it as a fundamental demand. The Leader has also made this clear to me in his own way, which of course means that he does not want his spiritual concepts interfered with just so that his Church can look modern in its organization.

At the same time, I have suggested with some insistence that the Church will stagnate unless it comes to terms with some precepts that have now established firm roots in secular society. I can provide two solid examples to buttress my argument. First, despite the healing qualities of the Church and its traditions, I have pointed out that its internal structures appear to limit the full flowering of women in the organization. Indeed, it is striking that the Barbados Spiritual Baptist Church has had a marvellous history and tradition of promoting the fulfilment of dreams and visions of downtrodden Barbadians. In a Spiritual Baptist sense, the call to dream has been an invitation to expand one's ambitions and to walk the universe, communicating with God and with the saints who have gone before. Passwords have been provided to help would-be dreamers circumvent the barriers to expansive pilgrimages in the secular and spiritual worlds. At the same time, women seem to be not invited to take the hand of Christ and soar as high as they can. But I believe that women will not accept this state of affairs forever. Their intelligence and experience have taught them that no man on earth can bind their dreams.

The second example I wish to provide is related to the organizational structure that the Church currently provides for the hearing of complaints against members. As things currently stand, the Leader may be complainant, jury and judge. I understand well that the process is founded on spiritual concepts that have to do with the fundamental notion that the Leader is charged with safeguarding spiritual ideas of what is right and wrong. I see no need to criticize that stance. Nevertheless, I take another line of argumentation. I note that the Leader has in fact been successful in helping Afro-Barbadians solidify their ethnic and religious identities. With this task complete, his Church members are now asking for their recognition as thoughtful adults participating in an organizational life in which they clearly have a stake. They are legitimately demanding a voice in what transpires within their Church. As I see it, this is not a call for a bending of the rules demanding adherence to God's word. It is simply the expression of a wish for self-respect, something that the Leader has taught them all about. In addition, hard as it is for the Leader to accept, while he is charged to establish the moral and religious tone of the organization, he cannot be above the ethics of simple organizational fairness.

Church members are now proud of their connection to the Spiritual Baptist heritage, which provides them with a religious identity that reinforces the ethnic identity into which they have grown in post-independence Barbados. I believe that they have moved beyond the classic Afro-Barbadian narrative of victimization to cultivating their new sense of a proud, liberated self with a uniquely direct access to God and to the saints of old. Abu-Rayya and Abu-Rayya (2009) have drawn our attention to the notion that, for some non-dominant group members, religious identity may equal or surpass the importance of ethnic identity in influencing the relationship between the individuals' concept of self and their well-being. This point is of substantial import and deserves greater study with respect to the Barbados Spiritual Baptists, as it is clear that Archbishop Williams set out to emphasize the interlocking significance of ethnic identity and religious identity as he went about preaching the fundamentals of the new faith to Barbadians.

These notions will play a dramatic role in how Church leadership approaches the task of solidifying the structures that will tighten up the everyday running of the group. Once that is done, there will be time to contemplate the next step of articulating the Church's mission for the coming decade or so. The work will not be easy. But it cannot be more difficult than what was done in the preceding five decades. The Patriarch has, by any measure, created a religious organization of immense beauty. Its profound impact on the history and culture of Barbados, coupled with its transformative effect on the psyche of Afro-Barbadians, will be fully appreciated only in years to come. At present, those who are close to him in the leadership must step forward and help secure the foundation of the establishment. It should not be permitted to deteriorate, as the Church now belongs to the patrimony of Barbados.

References

Abu-Rayya, M.H., and H.M. Abu-Rayya. 2009. Ethnic identification, religious identity, and psychological well-being among Muslim and Christian Palestinians in Israel. *Mental Health, Religion and Culture* 12:147–55.

Beckles, H. McD. 1998. Viv. In *A spirit of dominance: Cricket and nationalism in the West Indies*, ed. H. McD. Beckles, 1–15. Kingston, Jamaica: University of the West Indies Press.

Buturain, L. 2005. Materializing the mystery: Body imagery in Catholic visual culture. Paper presented at the Luce Colloquium, Fuller Seminary, Pasadena, CA. 16 February. http://www.brehmcenter.com/mediafiles/Buturain_paper.pdf (accessed 3 August 2009).

Chatfield, A. 1998. African independency in the Caribbean: The case of the Spiritual Baptists. *Missionalia* 26 (1): 94–115.

Clarke, A. 2002. *The polished hoe*. Toronto: Thomas Allen.

Cohen, E. 2008. What is spirit possession? Defining, comparing, and explaining two possession forms. *Ethnos* 73:101–26.

Cohen, E., and J.L. Barrett. 2008. Conceptualizing spirit possession: Ethnographic and experimental evidence. *Ethos* 36:246–67.

Duncan, C.B. 2001. Aunt(y) Jemima in Spiritual Baptist experience in Toronto: Spiritual mother or servile woman? *Small Axe* 9:97–122.

———. 2008. *This spot of ground: Spiritual Baptists in Toronto*. Waterloo, ON: Wilfrid Laurier University Press.

Editorial Notes. 1931. The Shouters. *Beacon* 1 (5): 2–3.

Elson, O.T. 2007. Gender-agency as communicated in the intra-interorganizational structures of the Spiritual Baptists of Barbados: A postcolonial account of cultural resistance. *Howard Journal of Communications* 18:15–37.

Fosshage, J.L. 1983. The psychological function of dreams: A revised psychoanalytic perspective. *Psychoanalytic Contemporary Thought* 6:641–69.

———. 1997. The organizing functions of dream mentation. *Contemporary Psychoanalysis* 33:429–58.

———. 2007. The organizing function of dreaming: Pivotal issues in understanding and working with dreams. *International Forum of Psychoanalysis* 16:213–21.

Glazier, S.D. 1983. *Marchin' the pilgrims home: Leadership and decision-making in an Afro-Caribbean faith.* Westport, CT: Greenwood.

———. 1996. New world African ritual: Genuine and spurious. *Journal for the Scientific Study of Religion* 35:420–31.

Griffith, E.E.H. 1983. The significance of ritual in a church-based healing model. *American Journal of Psychiatry* 140:568–72.

———. 1992. The psycho-social development and evolution of the Barbadian Spiritual Baptist Church. *Caribbean Journal of Religious Studies* 13 (1): 3–14.

Griffith, E.E.H, T. English and V. Mayfield. 1980. Possession, prayer, and testimony: Therapeutic aspects of the Wednesday night meeting in a black church. *Psychiatry* 43:120–28.

Griffith, E.E.H., and G.E. Mahy. 1984. Psychological benefits of Spiritual Baptist "mourning". *American Journal of Psychiatry* 141:769–73.

Griffith, E.E.H., G.E. Mahy and J.L. Young. 1986. Psychological benefits of Spiritual Baptist "mourning", II: An empirical assessment. *American Journal of Psychiatry* 143:226–29.

———. 2008. Barbados Spiritual Baptists: Social acceptance enhances opportunities for supporting public health. *Mental Health, Religion and Culture* 11:671–83.

Griffith, E.E.H., and P. Ruiz. 1977. Cultural factors in the training of psychiatry residents in an Hispanic urban community. *Psychiatric Quarterly* 49:20–37.

Guglin, T. 1974. The Spiritual Baptist Church of Barbados: A description of an Afro-Christian religion. Unpublished paper, prepared as part of the Colgate University programme in Barbados, September–December 1974.

Henney, J.H. 1982. Spirit-possession belief and trance behavior in two fundamentalist groups in St Vincent. In *Trance, healing and hallucination*, ed. F.E. Goodman, J.H. Henney and E. Pressel, 3–108. Malabar, FL: Robert E. Krieger.

Henry, F. 2003. *Reclaiming African religions in Trinidad: The socio-political legitimation of the Orisha and Spiritual Baptist faiths.* Kingston: University of the West Indies Press.

Herskovits, M.J. 1978. *The myth of the Negro past.* Boston: Beacon. (Orig. pub. 1958.)

Hoyos, F.A. 1978. *Barbados: A history from the Amerindians to independence.* London: Macmillan.

Jacobs, C.M. 1996. *Joy comes in the morning: Elton George Griffith and the Shouter Baptists.* Port of Spain: Caribbean Historical Society.

Jacobs, E. 2009. Hidden in plain view: Reconstructing historical memories of Africa through the Barbados landship. Unpublished manuscript.

James, C.L.R. 1993. *Beyond a boundary*. Durham, NC: Duke University Press.

Johnson, C. 2008. The end of the black American narrative. *American Scholar* 77 (3): 32–42.

Joseph, C. 1974. The trials of the Spiritual Baptist faith in Trinidad and Tobago. Address delivered at the laying of the Foundation Stone and Blessing of St Peter's Spiritual Baptist Cathedral, Gonzales, Port of Spain, Trinidad, 29 September 1974.

Laitinen, M. 2002. Marching to Zion: Creolisation in Spiritual Baptist rituals and cosmology. PhD diss., Research Series in Anthropology, University of Helsinki, Finland.

Lake, O. 1994. The many voices of Rastafarian women: Sexual subordination in the midst of liberation. *New West Indian Guide* 68:235–54.

Lovelace, E. 1983. *The wine of astonishment*. Caribbean Writers Series. Oxford: Heinemann Educational Books.

Lum, K.A. 2000. *Praising his name in the dance: Spirit possession in the Spiritual Baptist Faith and Orisha work in Trinidad, West Indies*. Amsterdam: Harwood Academic.

Morrow, R.C. 1983. On obeah, myalism and magical death in Jamaica. *West Indian Medical Journal* 32:4–6.

Mulrain, G. 2001. African religiosity in the diaspora: The Caribbean experience. http://www.afrikaworld.net/afrel/mulrain.htm (accessed 3 January 2009).

Palombo, S.R. 1978. The adaptive function of dreams. *Psychoanalysis and Contemporary Thought* 1:443–76.

Paton, D. 2009. Obeah acts: Producing and policing the boundaries of religion in the Caribbean. *Small Axe* 13:1–18.

Patterson, O. 1967. *The sociology of slavery*. London: MacGibbon and Kee.

Primus, P. 1993. Marian Chase annual lecture: Cultural bridges. *American Journal of Dance Therapy* 15:5–10.

Regis, L. 2005. Reflections of a legend. *Anthurium* 3 (2). http://scholar.library.miami.edu/anthurium/volume_3/issue_2/regis -reflections.htm (accessed 3 January 2010).

Rowe, M. 1985. The woman in Rastafari. In *Caribbean Quarterly monograph,* ed. R. Nettleford, 13–21. Kingston: University of the West Indies.

Sankey, I.D., ed. N.d. *Sacred songs and solos: Twelve hundred hymns*. London: Marshall, Morgan and Scott.

Seymour, S. 2006. Resistance. *Anthropological Theory* 6:303–21.

Simpson, G.E. 1966. Baptismal, "mourning" and "building" ceremonies of the Shouters in Trinidad. *Journal of American Folklore* 19:537–50.

———. 1980. *Religious cults of the Caribbean: Trinidad, Jamaica and Haiti*. 3rd ed. enlarged. Rio Piedras: Institute of Caribbean Studies, University of Puerto Rico.

Slinger, T. 2008. Church robbed. *Daily Nation*. 7 August. http://archive.nationnews.com/archive_results.php (accessed 9 January 2009).

Spiritual Baptist Church. 2008. Archbishop Granville Williams, in commemoration of the institution and investiture of the Patriarchate. Programme distributed at the service, 14 September.

Taylor, P. 2001. Dancing the nation: An introduction. In *Nation dance: Religion, identity, and cultural difference in the Caribbean*, ed. P. Taylor, 1–13. Bloomington, IN: Indiana University Press.

Walker, S. 1972. *Ceremonial spirit possession in Africa and Afro- America.* Leiden: Brill.

Ward, C. 1979–1980. Therapeutic aspects of ritual trance: The Shango cult in Trinidad. *Journal of Altered States of Consciousness* 5 (1): 19–29.

Ward, C., and M. Beaubrun. 1979. Trance induction and hallucination in Spiritual Baptist mourning. *Psychological Anthropology* 2:479–88.

West Indian United Spiritual Baptist Sacred Order: Popular hymns and choruses. N.d. San Fernando, Trinidad: N.p.

Williams, D.R., E.E.H. Griffith, J.L. Young, C. Collins and J. Dodson. 1999. Structure and provision of services in black churches in New Haven, Connecticut. *Cultural Diversity and Ethnic Minority Psychology* 5:118–33.

Young, J.L., and E.E.H. Griffith. 1989. The development and practice of pastoral counseling. *Hospital and Community Psychiatry* 40:271–76.

Young, J.L., E.E.H. Griffith and D.R. Williams. 2003. The integral role of pastoral counseling by African-American clergy in community mental health. *Psychiatric Services* 54:688–92.

Index